SCORPION CVR(T)

Scorpion FV101 Combat Vehicle Reconnaissance (Tracked) in British service 1972–2020

First published in January 2021

A catalogue record for this book is available from the British Library.

ISBN 9 781 78521 195 9

Library of Congress control no. 2018938913

Published by J H Haynes & Co. Ltd,
Sparkford, Yeovil, Somerset BA22 7JJ, UK.
Tel: 01963 440635
Int. tel: +44 1963 440635
Website: www.haynes.com

Haynes North America Inc.,
859 Lawrence Drive, Newbury Park,
California 91320, USA.

Printed in Malaysia.

Senior Commissioning Editor: Jonathan Falconer
Copy editor: Michelle Tilling
Proof reader: Penny Housden
Indexer: Peter Nicholson
Page design: James Robertson

Acknowledgements

Many moons ago in a previous incarnation, the present author was employed at MVEE at Chertsey where he was privileged to work with several of the principal actors in the early days of the CVR(T) story. These included the Project Manager, Colonel Richard Coombes MC, the Assistant PM Lt-Col Michael Norman RTR and Vernon Cleare, C Eng, FIMechE, who was responsible for the design of AFV suspensions and transmissions. Together we spent many days in the field during trials of early Scorpions. I shall never forget my first visit to MVEE Kirkcudbright where the local hostelry had 32 different malt whiskies to be savoured. The list of contributors to this book is legion and space precludes mentioning all of them and to those that I have overlooked I give my apologies and considerable thanks. For the sake of space, all ranks and post-nominals have been omitted with the exception of Maj-Gen (Retd) Paul Hanson CB, CBE, to whom I am indebted for the Foreword to CVR(T).

This is a book that relies heavily on interviews with CVR(T) users conducted over many years and I am deeply grateful for the information that they have imparted. The underlying theme that they have all stated is their deep-founded affection for CVR(T) as an AFV and for its sterling service over some 50 years: a true accolade to a remarkable AFV. I trust that this work reflects that accord between man and machine. Together they form a coherent team and an effective armoured fighting vehicle.

Alvis Ltd, Andy Brend, Andy Baker, Tony Cassar, John Clarke, Mark Coreth, Marcus Cowper, Les Critchlow, Charles Delamain, Alex Edmund, Bill Elspie, Darren Fern, Robert Fleming, George Forty, Christopher F. Foss, Mark Franklin Graeme Green, Andrew Greenwood, Household Cavalry Museum Archive, Robin Innes-Ker, Kevin Lambert, Hamish Macdonald, Derrick McManus, Patrick Mercer, Steve Mason, Brian Mitchell, NAM Templer Study Centre, Tim Neate, Ivan Nunn, Neil Palmer, Richard Quicke, RAC Tank Museum, Merlin Robinson, David Rowlands, Steve Sampher, Paul Simpson, Richard Stickland, Gary Stockwell, Pete Storer, Richard Taylor, the Merlin Archive, The National Archives, Pierre Lowe Victor, Robin Watt, Steve Webb, Tim Webb-Bowen, Martin Wickham, Frank Wood, Richard Wootton.

Photograph acknowledgements

Many of the photographs in this book come from private collections and from the Ministry of Defence under the Open Government Licence. Other photographs come from the archives of the following regiments: Household Cavalry Regiment, 1st The Queen's Dragoon Guards, The Royal Dragoon Guards, The Queen's Royal Irish Hussars, 9th/12th Royal Lancers, 16th/5th The Queen's Royal Lancers, The Light Dragoons, the Royal Regiment of Fusiliers, the Staffordshire Regiment.

And finally my thanks to the editorial and design teams at Haynes for their sterling work in producing this book, as well as my wife Jenny Spencer-Smith.

SCORPION
CVR(T)

Scorpion FV101 Combat Vehicle Reconnaissance (Tracked) in British service 1972–2020

Owners' Workshop Manual

An insight into the design, construction and operation of the Scorpion FV101 family of lightweight armoured fighting vehicles

Simon Dunstan

Contents

OPPOSITE A Chinook HC2 undertakes a Tactical Air Landing Operation exercise by lifting a Scimitar CVR(T) during training in Macedonia prior to the occupation of Kosovo during Operation Agricola in the spring of 1999. *(Getty Images)*

Foreword

Major General (Retired) Paul Nanson CB, CBE

The CVR(T) will always have a special place in my heart! Growing up, wasn't it the tank that Action Man deployed in? And didn't most of us have a Dinky Toy version somewhere in the toy box? And who can remember watching CVR(T) deploy to the Falkland Islands and even into Heathrow to counter the terrorist threat? During my service, I would be lucky to command CVR(T)s as a platoon, battle group and brigade commander, and I would serve in and alongside them on operations in the Gulf, Iraq, Bosnia and Afghanistan. As I look back on my 34-year career, I note that the CVR(T) has been there throughout and has been employed by almost every arm of the British Army – and of course by the RAF Regiment. It has served me – us – well and continues to serve; surely one of the most versatile and dependable armoured vehicles in the fleet?

As a close reconnaissance platoon commander in the late '80s and early '90s, my platoon was equipped with eight Scimitars armed with the 30mm Rarden cannon and the coax-mounted 7.62 machine gun. Petrol-driven, with its legendary Jaguar engine, it was the sports car of the battalion and, although a little tight, its crew of three loved it. Our job was to travel about 2km in front of the advancing battle group to find and mark the enemy, guiding the rest of the group into the attack. We spent many a 'happy' night marking routes through forestry blocks in the Soltau training area, or in observation posts overlooking 'Strip Wood' or the 'Obvious Crossing'! In 1991 we went to war; not against the Soviets, for which we had trained, but against Iraqi aggression in Kuwait. As you will read, the family of CVR(T) performed superbly on operations, taking the desert conditions in its stride. While we were slightly envious of the Warrior AFVs, with their luxurious living conditions and collective protection, there remained something special about being 'Recce'! In battle, the Scimitars and the Spartans were excellent; in the fight for the Pipeline crossing prior to Objective Tungsten, they packed enough of a punch while allowing us to stay agile enough to keep out of trouble. And I can only remember one vehicle breaking down during the entire campaign. Versatile, dependable, agile and reliable!

But the vehicle is only as good as the crew, and I was blessed with an exceptional platoon. We were a particular band of brothers, every member carefully selected and then put through rigorous training, reflecting the difficult nature of the job. Because we were so few, and required to work in isolation, we each had to know one another's jobs – be that gunner, driver, radio operator or maintainer. Of course we had to be skilled at the art of reconnaissance and all that came with it – navigation, observation, artillery target identification and forward air control, to name but a few. Reconnaissance soldiers, be they close or medium, are a breed apart and justifiably proud of their role and reputation.

So, I commend this book to you so that you might learn more about this legendary vehicle and the soldiers and airmen who man it. It is a story that is long, and all the more fascinating given the CVR(T)'s peculiar and essential irreconcilable design parameters from which emerged a highly successful reconnaissance vehicle, especially when placed in the hands of a skilled crew. It is the story of a vehicle that continues to be effective today, having not only enjoyed a long and distinguished career within the UK, but also as one of the most successful British ground weapon exports of the 20th century.

LEFT The Scimitar of Captain Paul Nanson patrols the desert after the end of hostilities of Operation Granby in the search for abandoned Iraqi weapons with Fusilier Holt driving and Lance Corporal Bruton in the gunner's position.

Introduction

General Sir Richard George Lawson KCB, DSO, OBE, KCSS
(when lieutenant colonel at the British Armoured Vehicles Symposium held on 23–24 June 1971)

CVR(T) operational philosophy

The CVR family is designed to cover the Light Armour requirements in the Central Region of Europe, on its flanks, and in areas away from Europe where it may be necessary for us to send troops at short notice. In Europe, where we are heavily committed to NATO, the requirement is for medium reconnaissance across the British Corps front and close reconnaissance for the battle group. Elsewhere, operations may stretch over the whole spectrum from internal security to limited war, and the ground may vary from the hot, sandy Arabian Peninsula to jungle or Arctic areas.

Although we can plan on some heavy armour being available in overseas stockpiles or afloat, there are occasions when either heavy armour is unsuitable for the country or it would take too long to arrive. This means that any AFVs we can airlift into an overseas area must be able to carry out, in addition to pure reconnaissance, the fire support and anti-armour roles. In the latter we feel that a long, stand-off, killing range is essential, since the protection that we can afford to provide on these light vehicles is bound to be minimal.

Let us now look in a little more detail at the various types of operations for which we require these light armoured vehicles. First – those under the general title of Cold War operations. We have had our share of experience at this game and know how rapidly the initial situation can deteriorate with demonstrations turning to rioting and internal disturbances escalating into full-blown insurgency. We have used light armoured vehicles in Greece, Palestine, Malaya, Borneo, Jordan and Aden, and continue at the moment with internal security operations in the Persian Gulf and Northern Ireland.

In this type of operation, the tasks set the crews of these light armoured vehicles varies from surveillance and long-range patrolling to setting up cordons, enforcing curfews and establishing networks of communications. And, as has so often proved to be the case, providing the best form of intimate and close support for the infantry.

In limited war the opposition may well be equipped with all the conventional weapon systems. In some areas the main forces may consist of tanks, APCs and artillery with air support. In other areas the main threat may be from infantry, either massed or, when deployed in close country, in groups specially trained for commando-type operations with little logistic support. At the higher level of military operations, these light armoured vehicles will be employed for the traditional tasks of armoured reconnaissance: carrying out close and medium reconnaissance, which in our opinion involves a very definite need to aggressively fight for information; providing protective screens to report, delay and to acquire targets for artillery and air strikes; and providing mobile direct firepower to deal with enemy parachute- or air-landed forces. In addition they will also be required to provide an immediate anti-armour fire support to our air-landed forces until such time as our own tanks can arrive by sea or in areas where our own tanks cannot be deployed.

In general war, in addition to an intensification of their roles in limited war, armoured reconnaissance vehicles will be required to carry out nuclear, biological and chemical monitoring and the surveying of contaminated areas. They will therefore need to be equipped with Radiac and chemical detectors for this task and will have to be designed to provide protection for the crews against the effects of nuclear and chemical weapons. To match the operational requirements set by this multiplicity of tasks and variance of environment, we have designed this new range of light armoured vehicles around three main characteristics:

- First – High-endurance reconnaissance capability.
- Second – Effective mobility, both strategic and tactical, with a high mileage capability and a realistic water-crossing performance.
- Third – Effective firepower, both as fire support and anti-armour.

Consideration of required characteristics

Those who have been employed in armoured reconnaissance consider it to be a subtle art, which demands a light touch and quick response. There is no question of charging like a bull into a china shop, or of squaring up to one's opponents like a heavyweight. It is more a case of probing, feinting and then backing off in the face of real trouble. For this we need a vehicle which is small, adequately armoured and agile, and we will have to rely upon its low silhouette, mobility and silent operation to get us about the battlefield.

Air portability. It is unrealistic to think in terms of carrying only one vehicle in a tactical transport aircraft such as the C-130. We therefore set, as I have already mentioned, a weight limit of 18,000lb (8 tonnes) to permit a minimum of two vehicles to be carried in each aircraft.

Armoured reconnaissance vehicles must be able to move freely and unobtrusively: to use ground inaccessible to the enemy's main force vehicles, and to maintain a high average speed – both on roads and across country. Only with this degree of mobility, will they be able to range far and wide to act as reconnaissance elements to our present-day highly mobile mechanised formations. To achieve this a speed in excess of 50mph (80kph) is essential.

Armoured reconnaissance vehicles must be good enough at crossing water obstacles to make this a realistic operation without concentrating above platoon level. While we

are not prepared to accept the limitations of vehicles which have sufficient volume to be self-floaters, they must be able to swim with the aid of flotation screens, and also be able to get out of the water once they are in it, which is by far the most difficult aspect of the problem of crossing rivers. We therefore ask that they be able to get in and out of rivers with steep slopes and then be able to swim at 4mph (6.4kph), once they are in the water. If necessary, we are

OPPOSITE General Sir Richard 'Dickie' Lawson KCB, DSO, OBE, KCSS, was one of the most distinguished soldiers of the Royal Tank Regiment. He is shown here as a major in command of the Berlin Independent Tank Squadron in 1961. His presentation on the Operational Philosophy of CVR(T) in June 1971 makes the only mention of rubber trees as a determining factor in the width of CVR(T).

prepared to accept some form of appliqué kits for propellers and sprocket winches rather than end up with a duck that performs well in water but only waddles when it gets on dry land. While our light armoured vehicles must be able to cross water, this should only be one of their many pastimes, and should not become the major mobility design criterion.

With our worldwide roles, we also found that it was necessary to set a limit of 7ft (1.83m) for the width of the vehicle so that it could motor through narrow village streets, move along the tops of dykes and pass between the lines of rubber trees in South-East Asia. Finally, having asked our designers for a vehicle that could go 50–60mph (80–97kph) on roads, 25mph (40kph) across country, climb hills, cross rivers and negotiate rubber plantations, we asked them for brakes to stop it and a set of reverse gears to be able to go backwards fast!

Chapter One

The CVR(T) story

In the 1960s the British Army initiated the design of a single multi-purpose armoured reconnaissance vehicle that was to be amphibious and air portable. When this proved impossible, a family of vehicles capable of undertaking many roles on the battlefield was introduced as the Combat Vehicle Reconnaissance (Tracked) that entered service in 1972.

OPPOSITE 02SP40 undergoes automotive trials at Long Valley. This vehicle was the first prototype of the FV102 Striker ATGW variant. The registration number SP was the FVRDE designation for Special Projects.

The other side of the hill

According to the publication *British Army Field Service Regulations* (1912), 'Time spent on reconnaissance is rarely wasted.' This military axiom has stood the test of time in the unceasing mission to see over 'the other side of the hill'. The role of reconnaissance troops is to discover the dispositions of the enemy and discern his intentions while relaying this information to the force commander as expeditiously as possible. Within armoured forces, there are two schools of thought as

to the most appropriate method to gain this intelligence – by force or by stealth. The former approach requires a well-armed and armoured vehicle capable of fighting opposing tanks on almost equal terms, while the latter a smaller, highly agile vehicle that possesses superior surveillance equipment but only sufficient firepower for self-defence. It is a function of each doctrine that has a profound effect on the design of an armoured fighting vehicle (AFV) for reconnaissance purposes.

The British Army has traditionally advocated reconnaissance by stealth. At the outbreak of the Second World War, the Royal Armoured Corps (RAC) was equipped with three-man, machine-gun-armed light tanks supported by close-liaison scout cars for reconnaissance within tank formations. As the war progressed and it acquired global dimensions, the British Army employed numerous types of vehicles from the contemporary cruiser tank, the A27 Cromwell, in the armoured reconnaissance

BELOW The FV601(C) Saladin Mark 2 armoured car was the quintessential British Army medium reconnaissance vehicle of the 1960s. It served in many conflicts that marked the withdrawal from the British Empire, from Aden to Borneo, and latterly for peacekeeping duties in Cyprus and Northern Ireland. Production of Saladin ran from 1958 to 1972 with 1,177 built. The Saladin enjoyed considerable foreign sales and was employed by 19 other armies and some are still in service to this day.

regiments of the armoured divisions, to the diminutive Daimler Dingo scout car, which served in almost every unit in the army. Such was the demand for a scouting capability within the infantry and other formations that a dedicated Reconnaissance Corps was formed in January 1941, since there were too few cavalry regiments to support them all. In the event, the Reconnaissance Corps provided a reconnaissance battalion for each operational army corps and subsequently every division. From El Alamein to Arnhem and from Caen to Kohima, a gamut of wheeled and tracked vehicles was pressed into service in the reconnaissance role while at the war's end, a plethora of prototypes was leaving the designers' drawing boards, several of them featuring multi-wheel configurations and mounting the same 75mm main armament as fitted to the majority of Allied gun tanks in the West; a tacit admission that reconnaissance vehicles must have greater firepower for self-defence.

In the years after the war, many of these wheeled armoured cars proved invaluable in policing the far-flung British Empire and in the 'brush-fire' wars that characterised the 1950s and '60s. Although Cromwell tanks

ABOVE The FV603 Saracen APC was the companion vehicle to Saladin. The Saracen was the first of the FV600 series to be produced given the urgent need for protected mobility for the infantry during the Malayan campaign. The first prototype was completed in June 1951 and two others were despatched directly to Malaya for field trials under combat conditions. Intriguingly, both Saladin and Saracen were designed to be no wider than 8ft (2.45m) so as to fit between the rows of rubber trees on Malayan plantations, whereas CVR(T) was supposedly to fulfil the same function but at just 7ft wide.

remained in the reconnaissance troops of armoured regiments into the 1950s, it became almost an article of faith in the British Army as to the necessity of wheeled AFVs for reconnaissance. This was reflected in the first armoured cars fielded to replace the wartime designs – the FV700 series 4×4 Ferret for close reconnaissance in 1952 and the FV601 6×6 Saladin for medium reconnaissance in 1959. A companion vehicle to the Saladin was the FV603 6×6 Saracen Armoured Personnel Carrier (APC) introduced earlier in 1953 to meet the urgent need for armoured transport of the infantry in the Malayan Emergency to counter communist insurgents. These vehicles proved highly successful in service but, by the early 1960s, Britain's extensive overseas commitments were proving too costly and to maintain permanent garrisons around the world became a prohibitive drain on defence resources. As an alternative strategy, it was proposed that troops were to be transported by air from Europe to trouble spots around the world in the newly acquired long-range transport aircraft, such as the Armstrong Whitworth Argosy and Short Belfast, before heavy armour and reinforcements arrived by sea. To support the air-landed contingent, an AFV capable of providing fire support and with an anti-armour capability was necessary, while, at the same time, itself being air portable. At over 10 tons, the Saladin was too heavy for this role in the contemporary generation of transport aircraft.

The quest for Light Armour

In the late 1950s, the Fighting Vehicles Research and Development Establishment (FVRDE) at Chertsey in Surrey was a centre of excellence for weapons development across the board. From the ongoing export success of Centurion and the design of its powerful successor Chieftain to the introduction of FV601 Saladin and the FV430 series of tracked vehicles, FVRDE had been undertaking numerous concept designs to meet the army's worldwide commitments to take on 'limited war' or 'brush-fire' type operations that typified the withdrawal from empire, such as Malaya, Kenya and Aden. With the introduction of the FV601 Saladin 6×6 wheeled reconnaissance vehicle in 1959, the British Army soon issued a requirement for a new generation of light AFVs.

At the Director Royal Armoured Corps (DRAC) Conference of December 1961, Lieutenant Colonel Richard Simpkin MC gave a presentation summarising the requirements of RAC equipment for the coming 15 years. These came about after a number of design proposals put forward following discussions between the User, the General Staff, the Weapons and Equipment Policy Committee and FVRDE, as well as several other interested parties. In the field of Light Armour, the need was stated for a lightweight air portable AFV (APAFV) with an in-service date of 1966; an improved reconnaissance vehicle for 1968

and a scout car of much enhanced mobility for around 1975. The APAFV was to be transported by Beverley aircraft to provide immediate armour support of air-landed troops across the world. In terms of firepower, the APAFV was required to undertake 'a substantial number of anti-tank engagements up to 3,000m and also of providing general fire support'. The vehicle was to have a high cross-country performance with high mobility, especially over sand, snow and mud, while being able to swim with minimal preparation.

The successor to Saladin was to become the basic AFV of armoured reconnaissance regiments with the following characteristics as stated by Colonel Simpkin:

A. It must mount one or more of a series of devices that will give it an observation and surveillance capability up to 5,000m by night and day and in all weathers.
B. It must have secure long-range communications.
C. Its road performance should approach that of Ferret as nearly as possible. It must have excellent cross-country performance and be a natural swimmer.
D. It is currently named the 'Air Portable Reconnaissance Vehicle' [APRV] and this shows the importance attached to its suitability for dropping from [Blackburn] Beverley and Operational Requirement 351 for a proposed strategic heavy lift aircraft.

Lieutenant Colonel Simpkin continued:

On the firepower side, we are asking for the capability of a small number of long-range anti-tank engagements. The APRV will also need a light weapon system for use against light armoured vehicles, aerial targets, soft targets and men. It must be silent both in movement and when operating its surveillance equipment. Protection comes a bad last in this list and the most we can hope for is once more immunity to small arms and shell splinters. The remaining 'A' Vehicles that the Armoured Reconnaissance Regiment requires must match the APRV in running gear and performance. We do not want a

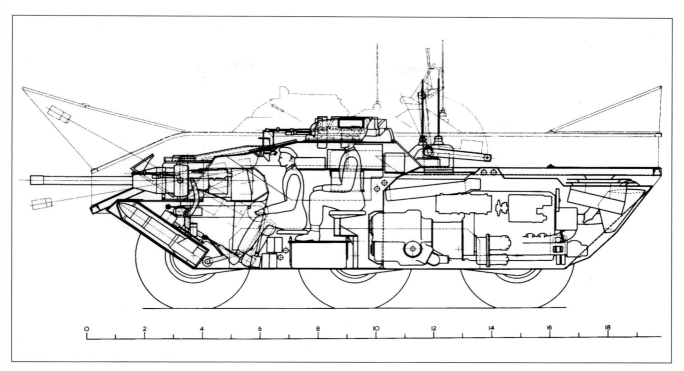

mixture of tracks and wheels. They must be a Command Vehicle, an APC and a version mounting a 20,000-metre surveillance radar. Whether tracked or wheeled, these requirements can be met from basic vehicles that will be in service or under development for other roles.

The final Light Armour AFV was a highly unconventional Scout Car that was to have the ability to fly over obstacles and rivers using the air cushion principle. With a proposed in-service date of 1975, this AFV was designated Ground Air Scout Car or GASC. Like all the above proposals, the GASC was at the cutting edge of technology given that the first hovercraft, the SRN1, had only made its maiden flight on 11 June 1959. Each of these projects necessitated considerable research before the actual specification was codified in a General Staff Operational Requirement or GSOR. Thus, the GASC was promulgated through GSOR 1009, the APAFV through GSOR 1006 and 3038, while the APRV was through GSOR 1010 and 3301. Each of these GSORs progressed through several iterations before a final specification was reached. Suffice to say, this prolonged and complex process is superfluous to this narrative.

Armoured vehicle reconnaissance

During design and development, the APAFV metamorphosed into the Lightweight High Mobility Tracked Vehicle Family, while the APRV became just the Armoured Vehicle Reconnaissance or AVR. Primary consideration was given to a wheeled variant but it soon became apparent that it was not feasible to integrate all the requirements of gun and missile armament, long-range surveillance and communications equipment while being amphibious and air portable into one AVR. The wheeled AVR housed a limited-traverse 76mm main armament in the forward hull, together with the Anti-Tank Guided Weapon (ATGW) launchers.

At a presentation in January 1964 of the project study on GSOR 1010, the forerunner of GSR 3301, the Royal Armament Research and Development Establishment (RARDE) offered a lightweight 76mm gun of ballistics similar to the existing L5A1 76mm mounted in Saladin. The reduction in weight of approximately 25% was effected by the use of high-yield steels in the major gun components. Designated the XL23E1, the new weapon was suggested for the armament of the AVR/FS, both wheeled

ABOVE During the 1960s and 1970s, both Britain and the USA developed many innovative AFV designs using the latest technological advances. Both armies required an amphibious and air portable reconnaissance vehicle with unprecedented firepower for a lightweight AFV, incorporating both guns for Fire Support and GW missiles for anti-tank engagements. The US Army adopted the M551 Sheridan with a combined 152mm gun/missile launcher of considerable sophistication. This Sheridan of the 82nd Airborne Division is shown at the outset of Operation Desert Shield in 1990 with the black HE rounds and the MGM-51 Shillelagh ATGW missile tubes on the ground beside the M-551. The British concept emerged as CVR(T) and both AFVs were deployed to Kuwait during the Gulf War of 1991. *(DoD)*

unit area it protects is almost identical to that of steel armour. However, as the aluminium armour plate is thicker than steel armour, it has greater structural rigidity thus obviating the need for as many crossmembers and stiffeners as used in previous light, steel-armoured AFVs. This both reduces overall weight and simplifies manufacture, while increasing internal volume for other components. Further research also revealed that the use of aluminium armour gave superior protection against fragment attack such as artillery splinters because of its greater areal density. Overall, significant reductions in weight could be realised in compact AFVs through the use of aluminium armour.

At the time, the British Army was constrained in the development of light armour by its commitment to the quadripartite agreement to produce a common Armoured Reconnaissance Scout Vehicle or ARSV with the ABCA nations – America, Britain, Canada and Australia. International cooperation in the design of major weapon systems was still in its infancy in the optimistic expectation that development costs would be shared among the various partners. As a rule of thumb, the costs escalate by the square root of the number of participants: thus for four nations the total would be double. As 'senior partner', the USA led the development of ARSV but none of the concepts found favour with any of the other ABCA countries, leading to the collapse of the whole project.

Simultaneously, the USA developed the Armored Reconnaissance Airborne Assault Vehicle (AR/AAV) that entered service with the US Army in 1967 as the M551 Sheridan. The vehicle had both an amphibious and air portable capability, being either air-landed from a C-130 Hercules or dropped by parachute. The Sheridan incorporated a sophisticated combined gun/missile launcher, firing both conventional HE rounds and the MGM-51 Shillelagh guided anti-tank missile. Sheridan incorporated an aluminium armour hull to reduce weight but even so, it tipped the scales in excess of 15 tons. Total production was 1,662 between 1966 and 1970 at a unit price of $330,000 (£128,405) and an overall programme cost of $1.3billion. Intriguingly, the Sheridan and the Armoured Vehicle Reconnaissance essentially shared the

and tracked. Furthermore, the AVR was to be powered by a multi-fuel engine with a power-to-weight ratio of 30bhp per ton that was quite unheard of in any previous British AFV design. For water crossing the hull incorporated a flotation screen that was erected by the crew to provide buoyancy while propulsion was provided by two hydrojets behind the engine compartment. This ambitious and complex proposal, however, resulted in a projected combat weight of 15 tons that exceeded the air portability limit.

It was apparent that there would have to be a significant reduction in weight if the AVR was to be air portable while providing more than a modicum of protection against small-arms fire and artillery fragments. Among the technological advances at this time was the use of aluminium alloy armour for AFVs: the first to be produced in quantity being the M-113 APC in 1959 by FMC of San José, California. The armour of the M-113 consists of the 5083-type aluminium–magnesium–manganese alloy that is relatively easy to weld but the weight per

OPPOSITE Due to the complexity of AVR, various other versions of the concept were proposed of six-wheeled variants for Fire Support, Anti-Tank and Anti-APC roles.

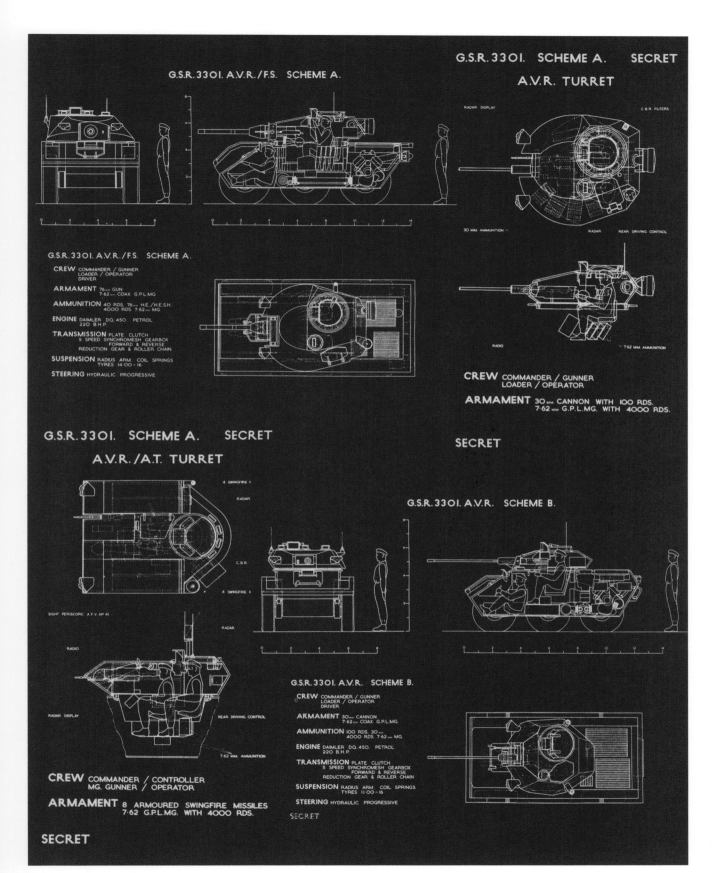

G.S.R. 3301. A.V.R./F.S. SCHEME A.

G.S.R. 3301. SCHEME A. SECRET
A.V.R. TURRET

G.S.R. 3301. A.V.R./F.S. SCHEME A.

CREW COMMANDER / GUNNER
LOADER / OPERATOR
DRIVER

ARMAMENT 76 mm GUN
7.62 mm COAX. G.P.L.MG.

AMMUNITION 40 RDS. 76 mm H.E./H.E.S.H.
4000 RDS. 7.62 mm MG.

ENGINE DAIMLER D.Q. 450 PETROL
220 B.H.P.

TRANSMISSION PLATE CLUTCH
5 SPEED SYNCHROMESH GEARBOX
FORWARD & REVERSE
REDUCTION GEAR & ROLLER CHAIN

SUSPENSION RADIUS ARM. COIL SPRINGS
TYRES 14.00 - 16

STEERING HYDRAULIC PROGRESSIVE

CREW COMMANDER / GUNNER
LOADER / OPERATOR

ARMAMENT 30 mm CANNON WITH 100 RDS.
7.62 mm G.P.L.MG. WITH 4000 RDS.

SECRET

G.S.R. 3301. SCHEME A. SECRET
A.V.R./A.T. TURRET

G.S.R. 3301. A.V.R. SCHEME B.

G.S.R. 3301. A.V.R. SCHEME B.

CREW COMMANDER / GUNNER
LOADER / OPERATOR
DRIVER

ARMAMENT 30 mm CANNON
7.62 mm COAX. G.P.L.MG.

AMMUNITION 100 RDS. 30 mm
4000 RDS. 7.62 mm MG.

ENGINE DAIMLER D.Q. 450 PETROL
220 B.H.P.

TRANSMISSION PLATE CLUTCH
5 SPEED SYNCHROMESH GEARBOX
FORWARD & REVERSE
REDUCTION GEAR & ROLLER CHAIN

SUSPENSION RADIUS ARM. COIL SPRINGS
TYRES 11.00 - 16

STEERING HYDRAULIC PROGRESSIVE

SECRET

CREW COMMANDER / CONTROLLER
MG. GUNNER / OPERATOR

ARMAMENT 8 ARMOURED SWINGFIRE MISSILES
7.62 G.P.L.MG. WITH 4000 RDS.

SECRET

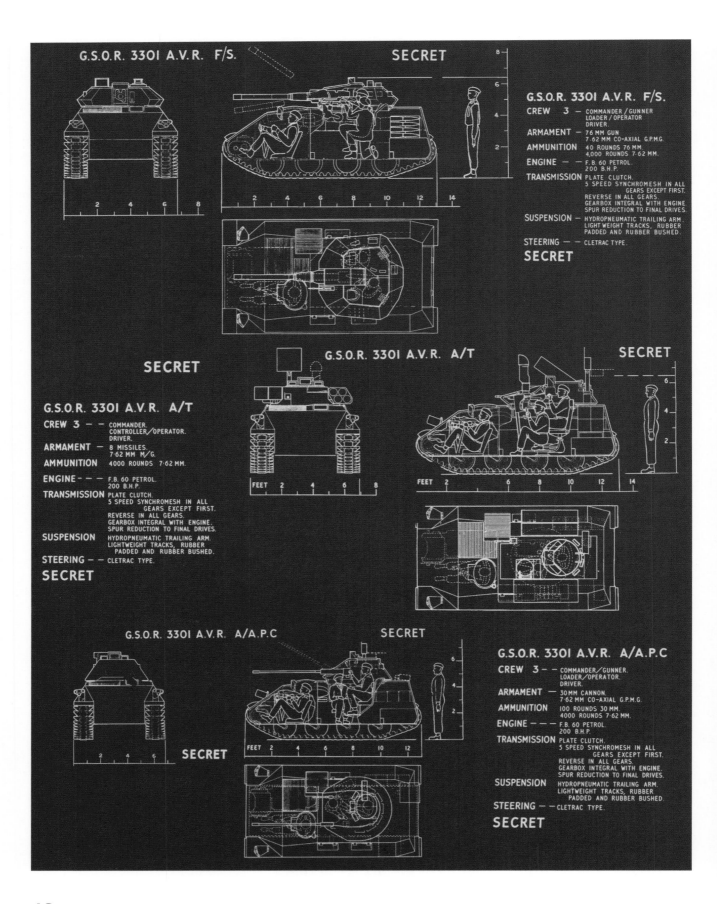

G.S.O.R. 3301 A.V.R. F/S.

SECRET

G.S.O.R. 3301 A.V.R. F/S.

CREW 3 — COMMANDER / GUNNER
LOADER / OPERATOR
DRIVER.

ARMAMENT — 76 MM GUN
7·62 MM CO-AXIAL G.P.M.G.

AMMUNITION — 40 ROUNDS 76 MM.
4,000 ROUNDS 7·62 MM.

ENGINE — F.B. 60 PETROL.
200 B.H.P.

TRANSMISSION PLATE CLUTCH.
5 SPEED SYNCHROMESH IN ALL
GEARS EXCEPT FIRST.
REVERSE IN ALL GEARS.
GEARBOX INTEGRAL WITH ENGINE.
SPUR REDUCTION TO FINAL DRIVES.

SUSPENSION — HYDROPNEUMATIC TRAILING ARM.
LIGHT WEIGHT TRACKS, RUBBER
PADDED AND RUBBER BUSHED.

STEERING — CLETRAC TYPE.

SECRET

SECRET

G.S.O.R. 3301 A.V.R. A/T

CREW 3 — — COMMANDER.
CONTROLLER/OPERATOR.
DRIVER.

ARMAMENT — 8 MISSILES.
7·62 MM M/G.

AMMUNITION — 4000 ROUNDS 7·62 MM.

ENGINE — — — F.B. 60 PETROL.
200 B.H.P.

TRANSMISSION PLATE CLUTCH.
5 SPEED SYNCHROMESH IN ALL
GEARS EXCEPT FIRST.
REVERSE IN ALL GEARS.
GEARBOX INTEGRAL WITH ENGINE.
SPUR REDUCTION TO FINAL DRIVES.

SUSPENSION HYDROPNEUMATIC TRAILING ARM.
LIGHTWEIGHT TRACKS, RUBBER
PADDED AND RUBBER BUSHED.

STEERING — CLETRAC TYPE.

SECRET

G.S.O.R. 3301 A.V.R. A/T

SECRET

FEET 2 4 6 8

FEET 2 4 6 8 10 12 14

G.S.O.R. 3301 A.V.R. A/A.P.C

SECRET

FEET 2 4 6 8 10 12

SECRET

G.S.O.R. 3301 A.V.R. A/A.P.C

CREW 3 — — COMMANDER/GUNNER.
LOADER/OPERATOR.
DRIVER.

ARMAMENT — 30MM CANNON.
7·62 MM CO-AXIAL G.P.M.G.

AMMUNITION — 100 ROUNDS 30 MM.
4000 ROUNDS 7·62 MM.

ENGINE — — — F.B. 60 PETROL.
200 B.H.P.

TRANSMISSION PLATE CLUTCH.
5 SPEED SYNCHROMESH IN ALL
GEARS EXCEPT FIRST.
REVERSE IN ALL GEARS.
GEARBOX INTEGRAL WITH ENGINE.
SPUR REDUCTION TO FINAL DRIVES.

SUSPENSION HYDROPNEUMATIC TRAILING ARM.
LIGHTWEIGHT TRACKS, RUBBER
PADDED AND RUBBER BUSHED.

STEERING — — CLETRAC TYPE.

SECRET

same basic design concept. Unsurprisingly, the US Army was very keen for the British Army to adopt the Sheridan but the 152mm gun/launcher system never found favour with the RAC, let alone the unit cost.

By the end of 1963, the General Staff decided that the combined AVR was 'too heavy, bulky, expensive and complicated'. A consolidated GSOR 3301 was issued on 19 August 1964. It stated that a range of AVRs was now necessary to fulfil various specialised functions, including basic reconnaissance vehicle; AVR Anti-APC; AVR Anti-Tank; AVR Fire Support; AVR Liaison Vehicle; AVR APC; AVR Command Vehicle and AVR Ambulance in both tracked and wheeled configurations. All versions were to share as many components as possible, including a hydro-pneumatic suspension system with low ground pressure for maximum mobility. This was to be achieved by a power to weight ratio of 30bhp per ton. In order to achieve such horsepower in a compact configuration, several engine types were investigated including gas turbine, Wankel, multi-fuel, compression ignition and petrol spark ignition. The latter was chosen in the form of a lightweight version of the Rolls-Royce FB60 engine. Even so, in its initial configuration it did not reach the desired horsepower specification.

While the wheeled variants were designed *ab initio*, the tracked versions of AVR evolved from the Lightweight High Mobility Tracked Vehicle Family. The latter was being designed simultaneously under GSOR 3038 that had been presented to the General Staff on 29 July 1964. This gave rise to numerous different variants, both wheeled and tracked, that defeated the whole concept of the original Armoured Vehicle Reconnaissance. However, the AVR was too heavy and bulky to be carried by a Blackburn Beverley or Handley Page Hastings when the GSOR specified that two AVRs were to be carried in a single transport aircraft or one in the airdrop role. Under Operational Requirement 351, the design for a strategic heavy-lift aircraft to supersede the Beverley and Hastings within RAF Transport Command had begun in March 1962. Designed and developed by Hawker Siddeley Aviation, the aircraft was designated AW.681 but with a payload of 35,000lb, it too could only carry a single AVR.

BELOW The whole concept of the Armoured Vehicle Reconnaissance (AVR) was predicated on the availability of a suitable heavy-lift transport aircraft such as the Armstrong AW.681. This highly sophisticated design was to have a STOL and VTOL capability. The latter was to be attained by incorporating the Rolls-Royce Pegasus turbofan engines that were developed for the Harrier 'Jump Jet'. The prototype was scheduled to fly in 1966 but the project was cancelled in 1965 and with it the fate of the AVR was sealed. The artwork depicts AVRs being unloaded from RAF Transport Command AW.681 aircraft at some notional Middle Eastern country. *(Artwork by Mark Franklin)*

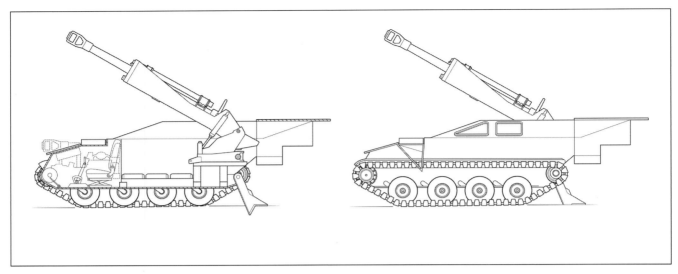

ABOVE The Lightweight Close Support Weapon (LCSW) was originally developed for the Royal Artillery after the demise of the FV300 series of self-propelled artillery weapons. The lightweight 105mm gun could be fired as a self-propelled weapon or dismounted for ground action with the vehicle acting as an ammunition limber. LCSW was designed to be airportable as a fire support weapon in air-landed operations. The concept introduced the four-wheel chassis and the front-mounted engine with the driver beside it that became a feature of the Lightweight High Mobility Tracked Vehicle Family (LHMTVF) and eventually Scorpion CVR(T).

Lightweight High Mobility Tracked Vehicle Family

In response to the original requirement of the Royal Armoured Corps for an air portable AFV, the General Staff finally proposed a complete range of AFVs that was designated the Lightweight High Mobility Tracked Vehicle Family (LHMTVF) that would be truly air portable with an overall weight limit of 5 tons each. The military characteristics of LHMTVF were issued in GSR 3038 that embraced the design concept of an earlier project for the Royal Artillery – the innovative Lightweight Close Support Weapon.

The basic variant of LHMTVF was the Infantry General Purpose Vehicle that was adaptable to a number of roles without materially altering the overall structure or shell of the vehicle. The roles envisaged included as a small APC, infantry reconnaissance and command vehicles. Such a variant provided highly mobile, armoured protection to specialised infantry teams such as pioneers; a command group or reconnaissance

elements with the latter incorporating a roof-mounted ZB298 ground radar, as well as radio equipment in the rear. All the versions had the engine mounted in the front offside with the driver beside it. Behind him was the troop compartment with the commander's cupola for all-round vision mounted centrally with vision and firing ports in the vehicle sides. The top of the compartment was designed with special folding roof and rear plates to enable it to be used to carry other weapons such as the 3in (81mm) mortar and the L6 120mm Wombat recoilless rifle. The Armoured Ambulance was a simple conversion of the basic Infantry General Purpose Vehicle with provision for two stretcher cases in the rear compartment. By convention this variant was unarmed.

The conversion of the General Purpose Vehicle to these roles could be readily carried out in the field. In the Wombat Portée Variant the weapon could be winched into the rear compartment for carriage across the battlefield. Once removed from the vehicle, the Wombat could be fired in the ground role. With the Mortar Carrier Variant, the rear compartment was used to carry the mortar tube, the mounting and some ammunition. The mortar base was attached to the rear plate of the hull to allow the mortar to be brought into action quickly by letting down the rear plate. Approximately 30×81mm mortar bombs were carried in racks at the rear of the vehicle. Both weapons' carriers had a crew of three, plus the driver.

The ATGW vehicle used the chassis and engine compartment of the basic vehicle

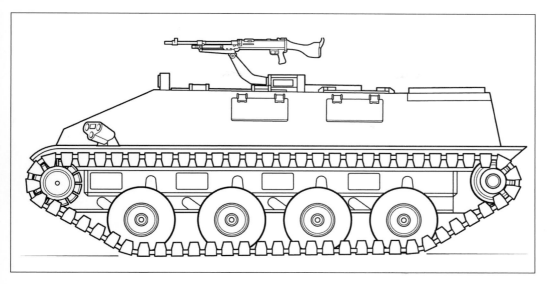

LEFT The Infantry General Purpose Vehicle of the LHMTVF was a compact AFV capable of being converted to various roles on the battlefield.

BELOW The 81mm Mortar Carrier of LHMTVF used the rear door as a base plate for the mortar for enhanced stability of the weapon.

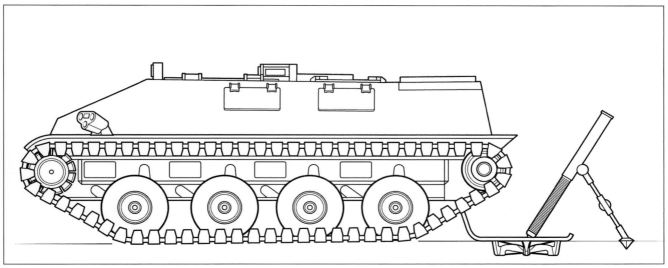

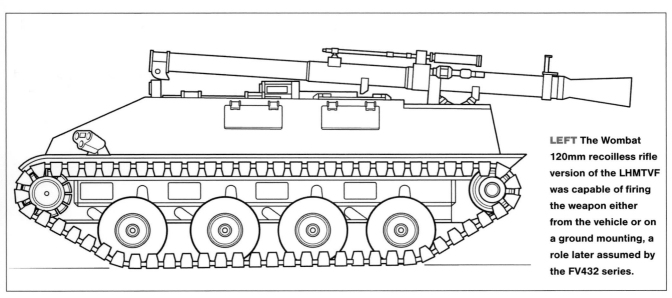

LEFT The Wombat 120mm recoilless rifle version of the LHMTVF was capable of firing the weapon either from the vehicle or on a ground mounting, a role later assumed by the FV432 series.

RIGHT The anti-tank variant of the LHMTVF carried 12 Swingfire ATGWs in four banks of three missiles with the commander and gunner in a sealed compartment behind them.

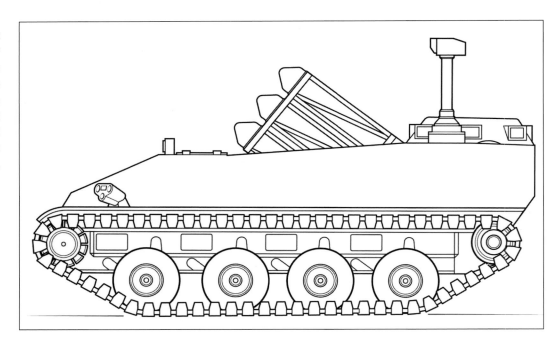

RIGHT The Convoy Escort variant of the LHMTVF was intended as its name implies to protect soft skin vehicles during ambushes as well as having an anti-APC capability.

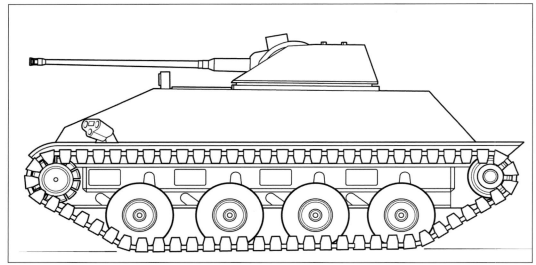

RIGHT The Armoured Ambulance variant of LHMTVF was a simple conversion of the basic General-Purpose Vehicle but without armament.

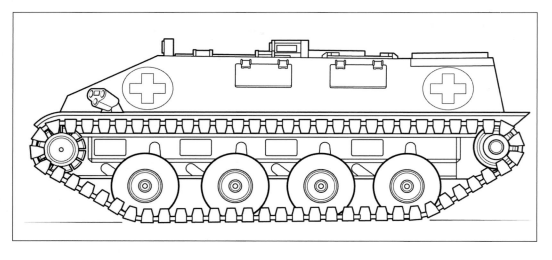

but the top structure of the hull was different. As with the other members of the family, the driver was seated alongside the engine but with a fireproof bulkhead behind him. The 12 Swingfire missiles were carried horizontally in the centre portion of the hull in four frames, each carrying three missiles. These frames were hinged at the rear and raised the missiles from their stowed location into the firing position as required. The commander and missile controller sat at the rear of the vehicle in a compartment separated from the missile stowage area by a fireproof bulkhead. An all-round vision cupola was provided for general surveillance while a long-necked periscopic sight mounted to the side of the cupola was used for controlling the missile. The Swingfire ATGW had a maximum range of 4,000m and was capable of destroying all contemporary Main Battle Tanks (MBTs).

The Malayan Emergency and Indonesian Confrontation during the 1950s and '60s prompted the requirement for a Convoy Escort Vehicle following the ambush of many military convoys on jungle roads. This variant featured a Hispano-Suiza A26 turret mounting a 20mm Hispano automatic cannon. This installation gave 360° traverse with a gun elevation of 75° and 10° depression. The A26 turret carried 1,000 rounds of ammunition in a continuous-feed system. This weapon system also provided a deterrent against low-flying aircraft, as well as being capable of providing effective action against lightly armoured vehicles and APCs.

While none of the LHMTVF was ever produced, many of these concept vehicles eventually emerged as the inspiration for the FV100 Combat Vehicle Reconnaissance Tracked Family. The FV103 Spartan assumed the function of the Infantry General Purpose Vehicle; the FV102 Striker of the ATGW Launcher Vehicle; the FV105 Samaritan of the Armoured Ambulance; the FV107 Scimitar the Convoy Escort Vehicle while the 81mm mortar-carrier and 120mm Wombat Portée roles were undertaken by the FV432 APC series. Similarly, the Armoured Vehicle Reconnaissance (Fire Support) never saw the light of day but its purpose and configuration is clearly reflected in FV101 Scorpion – the lead vehicle in the CVR(T) family: but that was yet to come.

Combat Vehicle Reconnaissance

During this period, the General Staff and the Royal Armoured Corps had refined the requirements for the next-generation reconnaissance vehicle. Mindful that the weight of the AVR had escalated due to the number of roles required of it, the General Staff decided in April 1965 to develop a family of two complementary vehicles – one armed with a 76mm gun in a fully rotating turret for fire support and one fitted with Swingfire ATGW launchers for engaging and destroying heavy armour at long ranges. Both were to be capable of acting as reconnaissance vehicles as well as being air portable.

All these factors were considered by the Concepts Section at FVRDE and it was decided to build an experimental vehicle designated TV15000 in order to test many of these technical features for Light Armour. Designed and built in 1965, the TV15000 made extensive use of aluminium in its construction and incorporated hydro-pneumatic suspension units that in the event provided little better performance over torsion bars for the extra cost, weight and complexity incurred. An extra wheel station was added to the four per side of the LHMTVF concept to improve cross-country mobility. At the outset, the TV15000 was powered by a Rolls-

BELOW The TV15000 was the vital link between the Armoured Vehicle Reconnaissance series and the CVR(T) family. Work on TV15000 began in June 1965 with it being scheduled for completion in March 1966, but the vehicle was rolled out of the FVRDE workshops on Christmas Eve 1965. The bare metal finish indicates that it was constructed with aluminium armour.

These two cutaways
show the evolution of
AVR FS to CVR(T) FS
within the GSR 3301
specification. The AVR
Fire Support shows
the influence of the
LHMTVF with four
road wheels per side
whereas CVR(T) has
an extra one for better
weight distribution and
mobility.

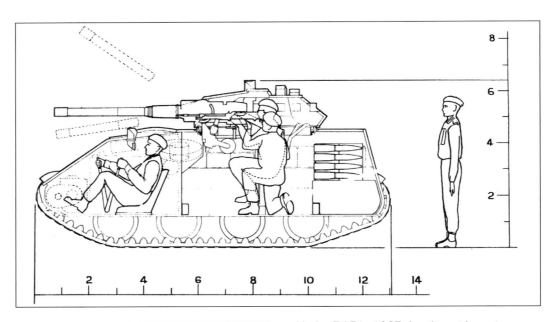

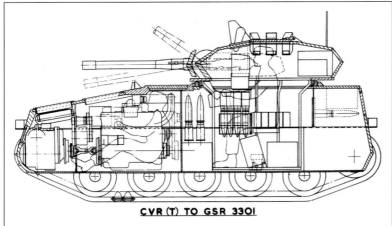

CVR (T) TO GSR 3301

Royce Vanden Plas FB60 engine with a gross output of 130bhp given that no new engine or gearbox could be developed within the tight schedule. This, coupled with specially developed lightweight aluminium track links, allowed the TV15000 to travel at over 50mph (80kph) – speeds unheard of for AFVs since the days of Walter Christie's innovative tank designs of the 1920s.

By now, the design project was known as the Combat Vehicle Reconnaissance (CVR). The weight limitation of 17,500lb became immutable to allow two to be carried in an appropriate transport aircraft. However, the AW.681 project was cancelled by the incoming Labour government in February 1965. In its place, the American-built Lockheed C-130 Hercules was procured, and it entered service

with the RAF in 1967. Another stringent parameter was the width of the vehicle, which was not to exceed 84in. It has been stated that this stipulation was made so that the vehicle could negotiate between trees in Malaysian rubber plantations that are supposedly 7ft apart, or the width of a fully laden elephant. In the interests of pure research, the present author has visited rubber plantations in Malaysia, Thailand and Vietnam where it is evident that there is no impediment to vehicles much wider than 7ft, the overriding impression being the appalling stench of unprocessed latex rubber. Indeed, the Saladin armoured cars of 4th Royal Tank Regiment and The Life Guards manoeuvred freely in the rubber plantations of Malaysia and Borneo during the Indonesian Confrontation of 1963–66. During their deployment to South Vietnam between 1968 and 1971, the 50-ton Centurions of the Australian 1st Armoured Regiment were able to fight in such terrain without difficulty. Such a width restriction might have been applicable to the particular internal dimensions of the transport aircraft then in service. However, this was not the case for the Beverley, Hastings or C-130 Hercules, let alone the putative AW.681. Furthermore, it is purely fortuitous that the CVR(T) fits inside the 7ft 2in width of an ISO container, since the latter's dimensions were only decided by international agreement in 1972 – long after the design specification for CVR(T) was formalised. Throughout GSOR

LEFT The mock-up of CVR(T) FS was unveiled at a presentation at FVRDE on 21 June 1966 and later that year at the DRAC's conference. It has all the hallmarks of Scorpion but retains the hydro-pneumatic suspension including return rollers that did not feature on production vehicles.

BELOW The TV15000, now with the registration number 04ED79, goes through its paces before a bevy of senior officers at Kimmeridge Bay on the east side of the Lulworth Gunnery Ranges with the Clavell Tower folly in the background. A variety of engines was tested in 04ED79 including a General Motors diesel and the Jaguar XK J60 that was finally chosen as the standard powerplant for CVR(T).

3301, there is no mention of any reason for the particular width limitation of CVR(T), so this aspect remains a mystery.

Furthermore, the General Staff required the CVR to be as quiet as possible, to be able to swim and be able to negotiate soft ground, necessitating a ground pressure of approximately 5psi or about the same as a marching soldier. Finally the General Staff determined that the two-vehicle family be expanded by a further four variants: an APC; an ambulance; a command post; and a recovery vehicle. All these models, together with the ATGW launcher version, required a superstructure at the rear for their various functions that established the

basic configuration of CVR with the engine, transmission and driving compartment in the front as determined by the LHMTVF. This common layout simplified production and therefore reduced manufacturing costs.

Since its introduction into service, the weight of the FV700 series Ferret armoured car had risen from 3.5 to almost 5 tons and more power was desirable in order to maintain its required mobility. In 1964, a standard Jaguar XK 4.2-litre petrol engine was fitted in place of the original Rolls-Royce B60. Extensive trials over 50,000 miles were undertaken without major failure that proved that the Jaguar engine could perform reliably in a wheeled AFV. Although the desirability of a diesel engine was

BELOW An FVRDE Scorpion prototype 01SP05, incorporating production road wheels, undergoes winter trials in Norway with the crew swathed in Arctic clothing that shows the problems of habitability within an AFV under extreme weather conditions and their impact on design parameters such as width limitations.

realised for its torque characteristics, range advantages and commonality of fuels, the calculated weight penalty of over 500lb was too great for air portability. Only one British engine fitted all the requirements and this was the 4.2-litre XK Jaguar engine, since no special tank engine could be developed before the proposed in-service date for CVR of 1971.

Since the width and weight were fixed, the overall dimensions of the vehicle were virtually determined because the ratio of the length of the tracks on the ground to the distance between the track centres is fixed within strict limits by steering considerations. This dictates that, to suit the steering ratio and the desired ground pressure, the tracks had to be about 18in wide, leaving 4ft for the hull width. As 2ft of space is the minimum required for a driver fitted out in Arctic clothing, only 2ft was left

for the engine compartment. To be exact the stipulated space required for a 90th percentile man is 25.16in (639mm) and as the actual track width is 17in (432mm) to which must be added clearance, plus two times the armour thickness of the hull plates, the internal width of the hull is 45.25in (1,149mm).

With the design parameters substantially set, FVRDE was authorised to build a mobile test rig to test the chosen major automotive components of engine and transmission. A second test bed was also built that essentially comprised the front hull section of CVR in order to check the efficiency of the cooling system, traditionally a weak point in British AFV design. Indeed, the first installation with its complicated drive system of twin centrifugal fans proved to be both costly and unreliable. A new development by Airscrew Howden

of a single mixed-flow fan gave the same performance as the twin-fan configuration but was far simpler to install while reducing overall power requirements.

The RAC also requested a higher level of armour protection that was needed for general warfare in Europe than had been envisaged for the LHMTVF. Accordingly, the weight limitation was raised to 17,500lb, which would allow two such vehicles to be carried in an AW.681 with its payload of 35,000lb.

ABOVE Following trials of the TV15000, a Mobile Test Rig of CVR was built at FVRDE that incorporated the Jaguar J60 engine and the TN15 transmission. Made by Self Changing Gears Ltd, the TN15 was a scaled-down version of the TN12 used in Chieftain that combined the gearbox and driving mechanism in a single compact unit.

BELOW The Mobile Test Rig 01SP66 was subsequently fitted with a mock-up turret to aid stability and mobility trials. The original hydro-pneumatic suspension of TV15000 was now replaced by torsion bars, together with the perforated road wheels characteristic of the Scorpion prototypes. The eventual configuration of Scorpion is now clearly evident.

By now the series was designated the Combat Vehicle Reconnaissance (Tracked) or CVR(T) to differentiate it from the proposed successor to Ferret, Combat Vehicle Reconnaissance (Wheeled), which was subsequently named Fox. Following the examples of Saladin and Saracen, CVR(T) was named beginning with S, with the 76mm fire support version being Scorpion because its rear mounted turret suggested a sting in the tail. An early suggestion for a name was Setter, but such an amiable dog does not have the same aggressive connotation as Scorpion. The others clearly reflected their function: Striker with its ATGW; Spartan as the APC; Samaritan as the armoured ambulance; Sultan as the command post and Samson as the recovery vehicle.

In addition, the General Staff had identified the need for a seventh member of the family – another turreted vehicle armed with a 30mm high-velocity cannon to conduct close reconnaissance. This variant was called Scimitar. In its original design configuration, the commander of CVR(T) was to act as gunner but after User pressure, following a feasibility study codenamed 'Cayuse' at the Royal Military College, Shrivenham, which indicated that his workload would be too great, this was changed to commander/loader.

While the Scorpion family fulfilled the British Army requirement for CVR(T), that for the Combat Vehicle Reconnaissance (Wheeled) was met by the FV721 Fox. A total of 15 prototypes of the FV721 were built by Daimler Ltd between November 1967 and April 1969 and the Fox was accepted for service by the British Army in July 1970. The 4×4 Fox has a three-man crew comprising commander, gunner and driver, and is fitted with a two-man turret armed with the same 30mm Rarden cannon and 7.62mm coaxial machine gun as Scimitar. Production of Fox was undertaken by the Royal Ordnance Factory Leeds, with Alvis providing the turrets. As a liaison vehicle, Ferret was to have been replaced by another version of Fox called Vixen.

The original in-service date of 1971 was

BELOW The wheeled school of thought within the Royal Armoured Corps was not to be denied their choice of reconnaissance vehicle resulting in the FV721 Fox Combat Vehicle Reconnaissance (Wheeled) that entered service in 1973. These two prototype vehicles of Scorpion and Fox display their relative dimensions to advantage.

delayed by over a year because of a number of factors. First and foremost was the abortive participation in the ARSV programme that precluded any simultaneous independent development because of a Treasury embargo that caused a delay of 12 months. A further 3 months were lost over the choice of engine and gearbox given the preferred option of the British Army for a diesel powerplant. Another three months were wasted when comparative development and production bids were sought from industry including Royal Ordnance Factories (ROFs), Vickers, Alvis and Joseph Sankey, the manufacturer of the FV432 APC. FVRDE preferred Sankey as the series manufacturer since Alvis was deemed to be too inexperienced in building tracked vehicles given their history of wheeled AFVs. A further delay of three months arose when the ROFs sought special consideration to maintain their production lines with CVR(T) but without success. However, they were given the contract to manufacture the CVR(W) Fox at the expense of its design parent Daimler that had produced the most iconic wheeled AFVs of the Second World War, forcing the company into liquidation.

In the event, Alvis Ltd of Coventry was awarded a development contract in September 1967 to produce a series of prototypes of CVR(T); the first 17 were Scorpion and the remainder the other 6 CVR(T) variants. Alvis undertook detail design work for the complete series using innovative manufacturing techniques and proven commercial components wherever possible in order to meet the strict cost limitations imposed by the Ministry of Defence. Completed on 23 January 1969, the first prototype was delivered on schedule, within budget and at the specified weight: a remarkable triple achievement in the development of any AFV.

There followed extensive testing across the globe with hot-weather trials being conducted in Australia (P6 and P7) and Abu Dhabi, and cold in Canada (P6 and P11) and Norway to prove that the vehicle could operate in extremes of conditions and temperatures of -25°F (-32°C) to +125°F (+52°C). A prototype Scorpion was also pressure tested in the British Aircraft Corporation stratosphere

ABOVE The first prototype of Scorpion was rolled out of the Alvis factory in Coventry on the date indicated but with an incomplete turret. The electrical bundle on the hull front was for the driving and IR headlamps that were yet to be fitted.

BELOW The first prototype Scorpion to be delivered to FVRDE shows the headlamps and inner IR night driving filtered lights together with the flotation screen around the lower hull, as well as a fully functioning turret except for the absence of the gunner's Image Intensification night sight beside the L23 76mm gun.

LEFT The Ministry of Defence Sales Team received its first Scorpion prototype in July 1972. With the VRN 47MS18, Prototype P13 undergoes trials at the Sovereign Base Area Dhekalia in Cyprus in late 1972 prior to a Sales Team demonstration to the Lebanese armed forces. The letters MS denote Military Sales.

BELOW During trials of Scorpion prototypes, problems arose with the combination of tracks and suspension given the absence of top rollers. The CVR(T) project manager, Colonel Richard Coombes, is shown driving a production Scorpion at high speed across country at the FVRDE gunnery ranges at Kirkcudbright with the turret crew of 17th/21st Lancers hanging on for dear life. The white figure at right is the present author filming the track play with a Bolex H16 16mm film camera. Note the RN Arctic convoy white reefer jacket that was the only concession to health and safety considerations in those days to prevent being run over by a speeding AFV.

chamber at Weybridge in Surrey to determine power losses at altitude.

In early 1971, a comprehensive review of CVR(T) was undertaken to examine problems arising out of prototype trials. The most significant was overall reliability, particularly of the engine, transmission and tracks. The life of the engine was found to be very much less than the expected 10,000 miles, although some improvement was assumed in the long term. Other problems included vision devices for the commander and driver, as well as turret crew seating that was prone to collapse at the most inconvenient time. To address these issues, P16 was modified in mid-1971 with the turret and driver's front plate redesigned. This vehicle incorporated, among other things, an enhanced commander's sight and mounting, new periscopes, better seating and stowage: the latter is a problem for all AFVs and particularly for a compact one such as CVR(T).

By the end of 1971, all three prototypes of Scimitar had been delivered and firing trials were under way. Such was the success of the trials that a production contract had already been placed. The main consideration was to increase the number of 30mm rounds stowed from the 99 as originally planned. A mock-up of a Striker fighting compartment with its five launchers, cupola and controller's sight was built in 1971. By the end of the year, safety trials were completed following two missile firings. Despite being the second vehicle as FV102 within the CVR(T) programme, labour problems and delays in providing sights were causing hold-ups in development. Three prototypes of Spartan were built on schedule and underwent trials with both Army Trials and Development Unit (ATDU) and Infantry Trials and Development Unit (ITDU). The major cause for concern was the heat and poor ventilation when closed down for extended periods. A single prototype of Sultan (P21) and Samaritan were completed in 1971, while the manufacture of a Samson prototype was in progress.

Between 5 February 1969 and 30 April 1972, the prototypes motored a total of 97,578 miles. Of this mileage, 24,179 were in general

LEFT Thirty prototypes of CVR(T) were produced with P1 to P17 being Scorpion given the initial order for such a number. P2, P7 and P9 became respectively P23, P24 and P25 as Scimitar prototypes. P8 was assigned to Belgium with P13 to the Overseas Sales Team. P21 was the prototype Sultan and P27 Samaritan.

roadwork; 26,760 on high-speed test track; 25,905 on rough tracks and 9,144 across country. Some 107 battlefield days were conducted and 3,560 main armament rounds fired. The mean miles between failure (MMBF) for automotive problems was 745 miles. Of the 131 significant automotive failures, 45 were due to specific design faults that were rectified before production began. If these are excluded, the MMBF figure was 912 miles.

The pre-production development costs of CVR(T) amounted to £3.81m; this included the design of the vehicle, some component development and all supplies and services. The charge of developing the L23 76mm gun and ammunition came to £335,000 but was ascribed to the AVR project for which it was originally designed. A similar sum covered the automotive and firing trials. The supply of 14 prototypes and immediate spares amounted to £1.3m with a further £1.5m for Post Design Services. The estimated unit price of CVR(T) FS at this stage was £50,500 (the same cost of Centurion in 1951) declining to £33,500 at

the height of production. CVR(T) was formally accepted for service with the British Army in May 1970. A production contract was awarded to Alvis on 30 July 1970 for 275 Scorpion and 288 Scimitar vehicles. The first production Scorpion was issued in January 1972. At the height of production in the mid-1970s, 40 CVR(T)s were built a month at the Alvis factories in Coventry.

In October 1970, a memorandum of understanding was signed between Britain and Belgium for the co-production of CVR(T), as well as the sharing of development costs. The Belgian Army ordered a total of 701 CVR(T) variants, including 153 Scorpions and 133 Scimitars, and production was undertaken at a British Leyland facility at Malines/Mechelen in the country's Flemish region. Belgium was responsible for the manufacture of the following: armour plate, gun mountings, gun mantlets and mountings, tracks, track adjusters, traverse gearboxes and road wheels.

The Belgian Army adopted all the CVR(T) variants, with the first entering service in 1973, until their final withdrawal in 2004.

BELOW One of the main tasks of FVRDE drivers was 'clocking up the miles' in exhaustive automotive trials such as here with Prototype P2 negotiating muddy ground at Long Valley in August 1969. P2 covered 5,303 miles of motoring out of a total of 97,578 during the automotive trials of CVR(T) up to 31 April 1972. Trials of Scorpion were conducted in Abu Dhabi, Australia, Canada, Cyprus, Lebanon and Norway.

ABOVE The largest user of CVR(T) after the British Army was the Belgian armed forces. During the Cold War, 1st Belgian Corps was assigned to NATO's Northern Army Group. Originally, the Belgian Army employed 153 Scorpions and 133 Scimitars in its reconnaissance units. These included 1st Régiment Jagers te Paard and Escadron 4th Chasseurs a` Cheval comprising two squadrons of CVR(T), each with three reconnaissance platoons, an anti-tank platoon with Striker and a Voltigeur infantry platoon in seven Spartans. A recce platoon was equipped with four Scorpions and three Scimitars; later seven Scimitars. The élite Régiment Paracommando also employed CVR(T) in its role as the Belgian Army's Rapid Reaction Force for deployment overseas. In that capacity, this Scimitar displays the national flag and insignia of the Paracommando during a peacekeeping mission in Somalia under UNOSOM – United Nations Operations in Somalia.

Chapter Two

CVR(T) anatomy and variants

From the outset the whole CVR(T) family was designed around a single platform, with a common chassis and automotive components for ease of manufacture and standardised crew training. This led to a family of highly versatile AFVs capable of worldwide deployment to meet a host of battlefield commitments.

OPPOSITE Festooned with vegetation, a Scorpion undertakes its primary task of reconnaissance by stealth while the crew commander observes for enemy activity with his binoculars during an exercise in West Germany.

LEFT A Scorpion of C Squadron, 17th/21st Lancers, speeds along a track during an exercise in BAOR in May 1974. The first production CVR(T) 01FD95 was delivered to the Technical Group REME in January 1972 followed by a second in February that was assigned to the School of Electrical and Mechanical Engineers (SEME) at Bordon.

BELOW The first unit of the British Army to be equipped with the CVR(T) Scorpion was A Squadron of The Blues and Royals (Royal Horse Guards and 1st Dragoons) from October 1972. The Scorpions of A Squadron are seen at top left together with various marks of Ferret, including Mark 1, Mark 2/3, Mark 4 and Mark 5, during a parade before Her Majesty Queen Elizabeth II as Colonel-in-Chief of the regiment.

The FV101 Combat Vehicle Reconnaissance (Tracked) Scorpion is a compact, highly mobile, air portable AFV. Designed primarily for battlefield reconnaissance, it is also capable of undertaking numerous other roles, such as fire support to infantry; counter-insurgency; road and cross-country convoy escort; force flank protection; route marking; and the ever-increasing demands for internal security ranging from patrolling airport perimeters to counter international terrorism to peacekeeping duties as part of a United Nations protection force.

Entering service with the British Army in 1972, the Scorpion superseded the Saladin 6×6 armoured car in the medium reconnaissance role but the latter was to continue in service for many years undertaking internal security and peacekeeping duties in areas where tracked vehicles were deemed politically unacceptable. Armed with the L5A1 76mm gun, Saladin weighs 25,536lb

(11,607kg) with a three-man crew, whereas Scorpion, with the more advanced L23 version of the 76mm gun and a similar number of crew, weighs only 17,500lb (7,940kg). However, much of this reduction in weight was achieved by the compact configuration of Scorpion that, inevitably, meant less room inside for the crew compared with that in Saladin. All members of the CVR(T) family share common automotive components, suspension and basic layout, which has significant procurement, training and logistical advantages.

Mobility

The driving compartment is situated in the front to the left of the engine with the combined transmission and steering unit in the nose of the vehicle. The driver has an adjustable seat with a folding backrest to allow access into the turret; either as a means of escape in an emergency or as access to the turret to use the commode beneath the

BELOW The driver's compartment of CVR(T) with the engine bay to his right and the radiators to his front with the oil cooler beside them.

**OPPOSITE FV101 Scorpion Combat Vehicle
Reconnaissance (Tracked).** *(Pierre Lowe Victor)*

1 Rubber mud flap

2 Oil cooler louvres

3 Driver's rearview mirror

4 Electrical generator

5 'Prairie snow' cover

6 L23 76mm Gun

7 Jaguar J60 petrol engine

8 Air filter

9 Exhaust outlet

10 External exhaust pipe shroud

11 Image Intensification night sight housing

12 7.62mm coaxial machine gun

13 Gunner's sight

14 Turret services box

15 Antennae tuning unit

16 Intercom control box

17 Gunner's hatch

18 Clansman VRC353 radio sets

19 OTIS (Optical Thermal Imaging Sight) bin

20 Commander's hatch

21 NBC pack

22 Rear stowage bin

23 Antenna base

24 Commander's sight

25 Rear idler wheel

26 Double road wheel

27 Fuel pannier below turret

28 Ammunition ready rounds stowage

29 Smoke grenade bin

30 Smoke grenade dischargers

31 Driver's position

32 Driver's control panel

33 Steering tillers

34 Generator panel

35 Torsion bar suspension

36 Sidelight and traffic indicator

37 Driver's external warning lights housing

38 Towing and lifting eye

39 TN15X Crossdrive transmission

40 Headlamp

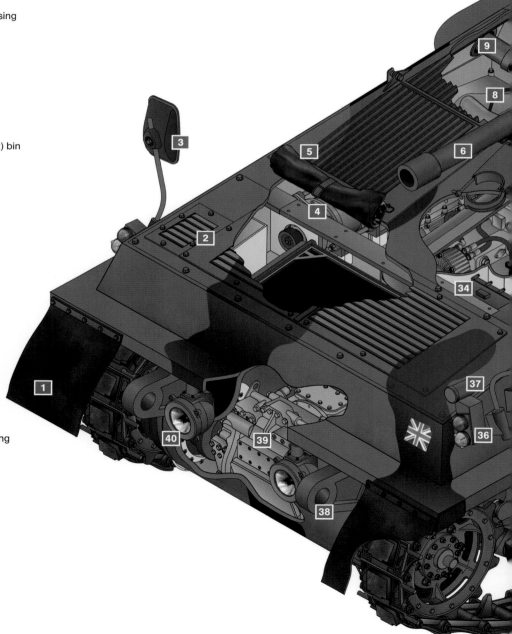

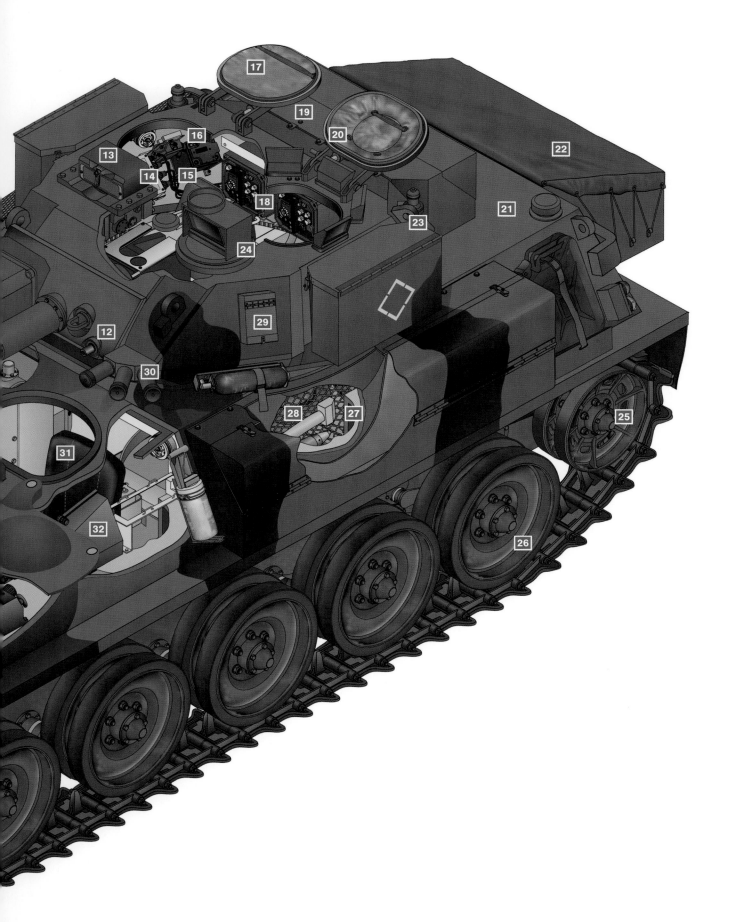

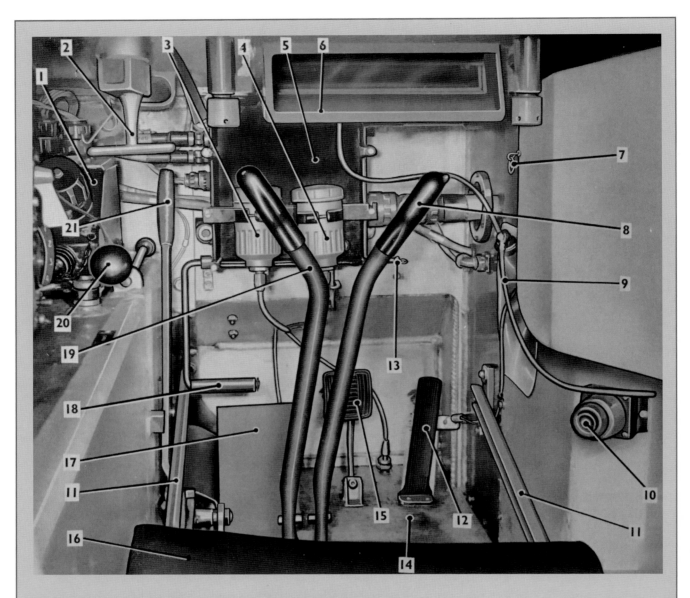

DRIVER'S COMPARTMENT AND CONTROLS

1 Master switch box/regulator panel

2 Driver's hatch catch

3 Footbrake hydraulic reservoir

4 Steering hydraulic reservoir

5 Generator panel

6 Day sight

7 Choke rod

8 Right steer tiller

9 Sight washer bag/reservoir

10 Washer hand pump

11 Seat rail incorporating raise/lower pivot and forwards/backwards slide

12 Accelerator pedal

13 Transmission compartment dump valve

14 Dip/main beam switch

15 Brake pedal

16 Driver's seat

17 Footrest

18 Gear change pedal

19 Left steer tiller

20 Forward/reverse lever

21 Ratchet handbrake lever

commander's seat when operating under Nuclear Biological Chemical (NBC) conditions; a procedure that was nigh on impossible in reality, so the driver was also provided with an interesting device known as the 'Beresford funnel'. Tucked in the hull sponson to the driver's left is the main instrument panel that is difficult to be seen when driving with his head out. The driver steers the vehicle using tillers. Gear changing is done with the left foot, while the right operates the accelerator and brakes. The GCP (Gear Change Pedal) is a pivot pedal bolted on the left-hand wall. Heel clicking down changes gears up, and toe clicking downwards changes the gears down the gearbox. There is a single wide-angle

ABOVE AND LEFT
Driver's control panel: the engine warning lights on the control panel were difficult to see when the driver had his hatch open and his head out. Accordingly, three of these were duplicated in a small housing mounted on the left front hull to indicate coolant temperature, oil pressure and a generator warning light.

periscope for driving while closed down, which can be replaced by a Pilkington passive image intensification periscope for driving at night.

The CVR(T) series is powered by the Jaguar J60 4.2-litre, six-cylinder, overhead valve (OHV), spark ignition engine with a single Marcus carburettor. It has a compression ratio reduced from 9.1 to 7.75:1 to run on military grades of petrol, which also reduces its gross output from 265bhp to 195bhp at 5,000rpm. With a combat weight of 7.8 tons, this results in a power-to-weight ratio of 24.32bhp per ton (17.85k/tonne) at a nominal ground pressure of 5psi (0.35kg/cm^2), giving both high acceleration and agility while enabling Scorpion to negotiate soft ground impassable to most other tracked vehicles of its generation. The maximum speed is approximately 50mph (80kph) and

an acceleration from rest to 30mph (48kph) in 16secs is possible. The Jaguar engine – the same one that powered the E-Type sports car – is a well-proven unit in regular commercial production, which makes it available at a more reasonable price than a specially produced military engine. A further point in its favour is its low noise level.

The British Army originally asked for a diesel engine. Unfortunately, no suitable engine was available within the development timescale. The General Motors two-stroke 4-53T turbocharged diesel engine underwent investigation, including an experimental installation in a test vehicle but, compared with the gasoline engine, it proved to be too noisy, created more vibration, was appreciably heavier, more costly and required further development before it would become acceptable.

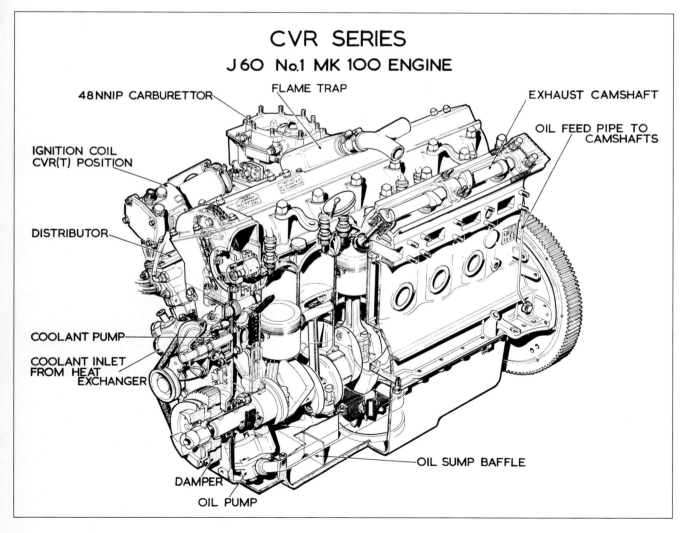

CVR SERIES
J60 No.1 MK 100 ENGINE

48NNIP CARBURETTOR

FLAME TRAP

EXHAUST CAMSHAFT

OIL FEED PIPE TO CAMSHAFTS

IGNITION COIL CVR(T) POSITION

DISTRIBUTOR

COOLANT PUMP

COOLANT INLET FROM HEAT EXCHANGER

OIL SUMP BAFFLE

DAMPER

OIL PUMP

The drive from the engine is transmitted through a centrifugal clutch, thereby eliminating the need for a clutch pedal, to the Merritt-Wilson TN15X transmission made by the company Self-Changing Gears. Derived from the design used in Chieftain, the TN15X comprises a semi-automatic, hot-shift, epicyclic gearbox with seven speeds, in both forward and reverse. It also features a triple differential steering system, controlled by hydraulically applied disc brakes operated by the driver's tillers. The radii of turns differ with the gear ratio selected and a facility for a pivot turn is incorporated. In a highly mobile vehicle such as Scorpion, it is important that the characteristics of the steering system are such that the stability of the vehicle cannot be jeopardised when turning at any speed. The transmission provides minimum turning circle radii in each gear, consistent with the speed at which the vehicle is likely to be travelling.

Although relatively simple to drive for a tracked vehicle, Scorpion does have its foibles, particularly when changing down from fourth gear to third because, in the hands of an inexperienced driver, the vehicle tends to nosedive sharply, much to the discomfort of the turret crew. The single epicyclic reduction gear final drives transmit power to the front mounted sprockets where some 70% of the engine power is available indicating the high efficiency of the system. For engine cooling, a single 12in (305mm) mixed-flow fan by Airscrew Howden draws in air through the radiator over the transmission, then over the engine and out through the louvres *above* the engine decks. This system is significantly quieter than other types and particularly suitable, therefore, for a reconnaissance vehicle. Trials had shown that the vehicle can operate in ambient temperatures of up to 125°F (52°C): temperatures that were repeatedly experienced in Afghanistan to the detriment of both vehicles and crews.

OPPOSITE The Merritt-Wilson TN15X transmission of a Scorpion is replaced by REME technicians with the aid of an American wrecker and its team.

BELOW CVR(T) cooling system.

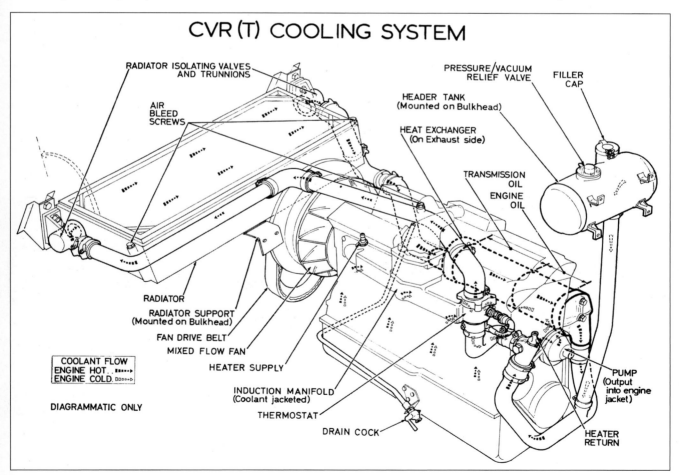

CVR (T) COOLING SYSTEM

RADIATOR ISOLATING VALVES AND TRUNNIONS

AIR BLEED SCREWS

PRESSURE/VACUUM RELIEF VALVE

FILLER CAP

HEADER TANK (Mounted on Bulkhead)

HEAT EXCHANGER (On Exhaust side)

TRANSMISSION OIL

ENGINE OIL

RADIATOR

RADIATOR SUPPORT (Mounted on Bulkhead)

FAN DRIVE BELT

MIXED FLOW FAN

HEATER SUPPLY

INDUCTION MANIFOLD (Coolant jacketed)

THERMOSTAT

DRAIN COCK

PUMP (Output into engine jacket)

HEATER RETURN

COOLANT FLOW
ENGINE HOT
ENGINE COLD

DIAGRAMMATIC ONLY

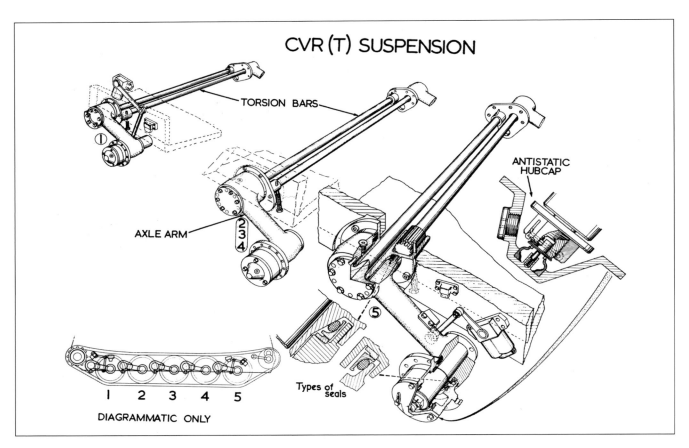

CVR (T) SUSPENSION

TORSION BARS

AXLE ARM

ANTISTATIC HUBCAP

2
3
4

⑤

Types of seals

1 2 3 4 5

DIAGRAMMATIC ONLY

ABOVE CVR(T) suspension.

CVR(T) is mounted on a transverse trailing arm torsion bar suspension system with five twin aluminium road wheels on each side. Dampers are fitted on the front and rear wheel stations and a vertical wheel movement of 11.8in (300mm) from bump to rebound is possible that gives a comparatively comfortable ride across country. The design of the torsion bars is a little unusual: they upset at one end to provide a flange so that it can be bolted to the aluminium axle arm, since obviously a splined connection cannot be used.

When designing any tracked vehicle it is of prime importance to produce a track that is light in weight, as this can affect vehicle performance considerably. At any given time only approximately a third of the track length is actually working, while the remaining two thirds, in effect, represents a weight penalty that is unavoidably carried, and so should be kept to a minimum. The track designed for CVR(T) is of skeleton construction with a width of 430mm (17in) and a pitch of 115mm (4.5in). The whole track accounts for 9% of the vehicle weight. Because Scorpion is primarily

a reconnaissance vehicle, attention has been paid to details that contribute to the reduction of noise. The track incorporates rubber-bushed hinge pins, rubber pads and a rubbered wheel path. A polyurethane track support ring is fitted in the sprocket assembly to damp out noise arising from the track/sprocket engagement. Noise-reduction measures have also eliminated the tell-tale signature clatter of the tracked vehicle, making the type of vehicle difficult to identify by sound alone – an important feature for a reconnaissance vehicle. Track life depends on a number of factors – including terrain and maintenance – but the design specification of 3,000 miles (4,800km) of mixed road and cross-country running was never achieved in service. Similarly, particular attention was paid to the design of the road wheels. The solid rubber-tyred wheels make a considerable contribution to noise reduction and also perform a very necessary function in damping out the vibrations in combination with the rubber-faced track links.

The fuel tank capacity of over 400 litres (90 Imperial gallons) is formed naturally by the rear bulkhead and the rear hull plates and gives the vehicle a road range approaching 560km (350 miles). A rubber bag tank is fitted in this compartment that helps to contain the fuel in the event of hull damage. The Scorpion can ford to a depth of 1m without preparation but to enhance tactical mobility further, all members of the family can be fitted with a collapsible flotation screen around the top of the hull. In theory, this can be erected in under 10 minutes and the vehicle can propel and steer itself across rivers and lakes using its tracks at a maximum speed of 3.6mph (6.5kph).

Firepower

The fighting compartment of Scorpion is located at the rear of the hull in a fully rotating turret with a ring diameter of 55in (1.4m). The commander is positioned on the left and the gunner on the right. Between them is the L23A1 medium velocity 76mm gun which, through the use of higher-tensile strength steel, is some 25% lighter than the L5A1 version installed in the Saladin

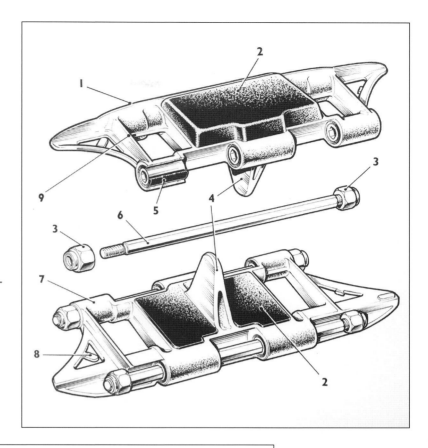

ABOVE Grouser, spud, horn, pad, web, track pin nut were the key points to remember of the CVR(T) track link.

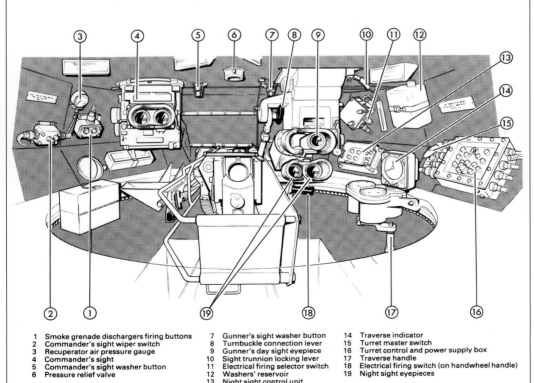

1	Smoke grenade dischargers firing buttons	7	Gunner's sight washer button	14	Traverse indicator
2	Commander's sight wiper switch	8	Turnbuckle connection lever	15	Turret master switch
3	Recuperator air pressure gauge	9	Gunner's day sight eyepiece	16	Turret control and power supply box
4	Commander's sight	10	Sight trunnion locking lever	17	Traverse handle
5	Commander's sight washer button	11	Electrical firing selector switch	18	Electrical firing switch (on handwheel handle)
6	Pressure relief valve	12	Washers' reservoir	19	Night sight eyepieces
		13	Night sight control unit		

LEFT Scorpion fighting compartment.

armoured car. Developed by the RARDE and manufactured by the ROFs, the 76mm gun is of orthodox design, having a vertical sliding breech, and loaded with fixed-type ammunition. Firing may be electromechanical (using a solenoid), or mechanical (by way of a foot pedal). The recoil is approximately 28cm and the gun is returned to the firing position by hydro-pneumatic recuperator. During run-out, the breech is opened by a semi-automatic cam and the spent case ejected; the breech remains open for reloading.

Forty rounds of 76mm ammunition are carried in a mix of HESH (High-Explosive Squash Head); HE; Smoke; Illuminating and Canister. The L29 HESH round is the primary round for defeating medium armour, but it is also highly effective against buildings, concrete emplacements and other battlefield targets, while its lethality against troops in the open or under light cover is only marginally less than conventional HE.

The main armament of the Scorpion has a maximum elevation of 35° and a depression of 10° throughout the full range of turret traverse. To save cost and weight, the gun controls and turret traverse are manually operated, which is one of the most unpopular aspects of Scorpion with its crews. A clinometer and traverse indicator are fitted as standard. Secondary armament is a 7.62mm L43A1 machine gun mounted coaxially to the left of the 76mm gun. Some 3,000 rounds of 7.62mm ammunition are carried and, in addition to being used in the normal suppressive fire role, the L431 can be used as a ranging gun for the main armament out to 1,600m, although the 'Eyeball Mark I' is the usual method of range estimation for direct fire. Mounted on each side of the forward part of the turret is a bank of three (later four) electrically operated smoke grenade dischargers to produce a smokescreen behind which the Scorpion can retreat to cover an emergency.

BELOW Turret view.

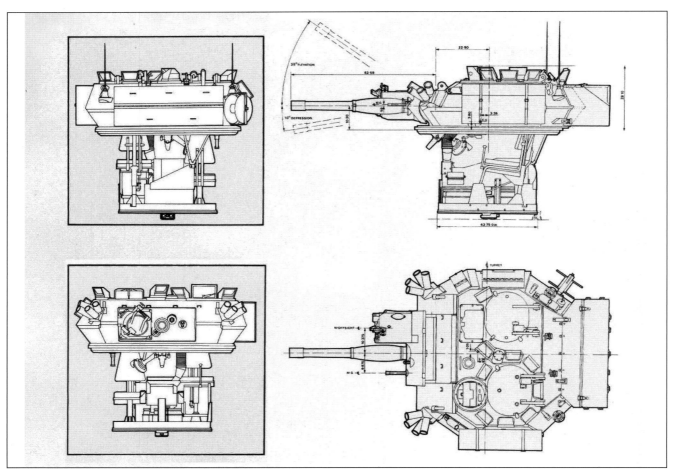

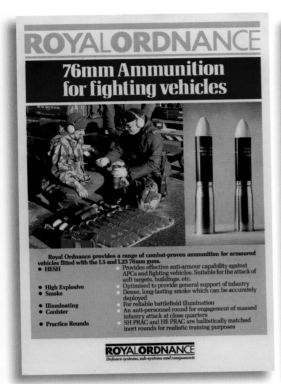

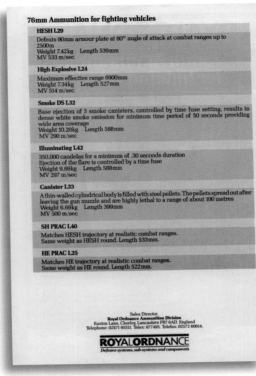

ROYAL ORDNANCE

76mm Ammunition for fighting vehicles

Royal Ordnance provides a range of combat-proven ammunition for armoured vehicles fitted with the L5 and L23 76mm guns.

- HESH
- High Explosive
- Smoke
- Illuminating
- Canister
- Practice Rounds

- Provides effective anti-armour capability against APCs and fighting vehicles. Suitable for the attack of soft targets, buildings, etc.
- Optimised to provide general support of infantry
- Dense, long-lasting smoke which can be accurately deployed
- For reliable battlefield illumination
- An anti-personnel round for engagement of massed infantry attack at close quarters
- SH PRAC and HE PRAC are ballistically matched inert rounds for realistic training purposes

ROYAL ORDNANCE
Defence systems, sub-systems and components

76mm Ammunition for fighting vehicles

HESH L29
Defeats 90mm armour plate at 60° angle of attack at combat ranges up to 2500m
Weight 7.42kg   Length 539mm
MV 533 m/sec

High Explosive L24
Maximum effective range 6900mm
Weight 7.34kg   Length 527mm
MV 514 m/sec

Smoke DS L32
Base ejection of 3 smoke canisters, controlled by time fuse setting, results in dense white smoke omission for minimum time period of 50 seconds providing wide area coverage
Weight 10.20kg   Length 588mm
MV 290 m/sec

Illuminating L42
350,000 candelas for a minimum of .30 seconds duration
Ejection of the flare is controlled by a time fuse
Weight 9.69kg   Length 588mm
MV 297 m/sec

Canister L33
A thin-walled cylindrical body is filled with steel pellets. The pellets spread out after leaving the gun muzzle and are highly lethal to a range of about 100 metres
Weight 6.69kg   Length 399mm
MV 500 m/sec

SH PRAC L40
Matches HESH trajectory at realistic combat ranges.
Same weight as HESH round. Length 533mm.

HE PRAC L25
Matches HE trajectory at realistic combat ranges.
Same weight as HE round. Length 522mm.

Sales Director,
Royal Ordnance Ammunition Division
Euxton Lane, Chorley, Lancashire PR7 6AD. England
Telephone: 02571 65511. Telex: 677495. Telefax: 02572 60614.

ROYAL ORDNANCE
Defence systems, sub-systems and components

LEFT The L23A1 76mm gun fires a wide range of projectiles as shown in this Royal Ordnance brochure, although the L24 HE round seems somewhat limited with its indicated range of 6,900mm or just 23ft.

BELOW Every variant in the CVR(T) range is equipped with smoke dischargers as a self-protection measure. Manufactured by Helio Defence Systems, the No 12 launcher fires 66mm WP grenades to create an instant smokescreen.

RIGHT The inner workings of the Rank Precision Industries SPAV L3A1 Image Intensification sight are seen in this view of an early production Scorpion.

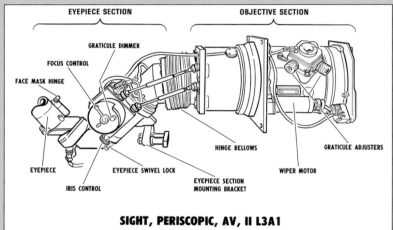

EYEPIECE SECTION

OBJECTIVE SECTION

GRATICULE DIMMER

FOCUS CONTROL

FACE MASK HINGE

EYEPIECE

IRIS CONTROL

EYEPIECE SWIVEL LOCK

HINGE BELLOWS

EYEPIECE SECTION MOUNTING BRACKET

WIPER MOTOR

GRATICULE ADJUSTERS

SIGHT, PERISCOPIC, AV, II L3A1

CVR(T) SIGHT

During the early 1980s, the trend was to procuring thermal imaging (TI) sights for AFVs that gave greatly improved performance by day and night, both for surveillance and firing engagements. At that time, the only CVR(T) to have a TI capability was Striker. In 1984, the British Army adopted the Observers Thermal Imaging Sight (OTIS) for use by Royal Artillery and infantry, as well as the Royal Armoured Corps. Initially, OTIS was issued on a scale of two per medium reconnaissance troop. However, OTIS did have some distinct tactical drawbacks. First and foremost, it had to be mounted atop the turret, thus exposing the operator, and it could neither be used with the vehicle in motion nor when firing the main armament. A further problem of OTIS was that it took up vital stowage space in the rear turret bin when not mounted. Interestingly, ATDU managed to fit OTIS within the existing II housing to overcome these problems but this was not pursued on the grounds of cost.

LEFT Sight, periscopic, AV, II L3A1.

BELOW The Scorpion incorporated the L3A1 image intensification sight with its characteristic circular objective lens while that of the L2A1 was square. The green image became more granular and hazy as the light level diminished so on a clear night on the Hohne ranges, gunnery was straightforward but in a dank, dark German forest even navigation became a problem. However, the judicious use of the IR headlamps and the II sight allowed the driver to be guided through the trees although depth perception was minimal.

BELOW While the OTIS Observation Thermal Imaging Sight gave much improved performance over its predecessor, the mounting above the commander's primary vision sight was ungainly and required precise alignment. OTIS was not to be used when the CVR(T) was in motion nor when the main armament was fired.

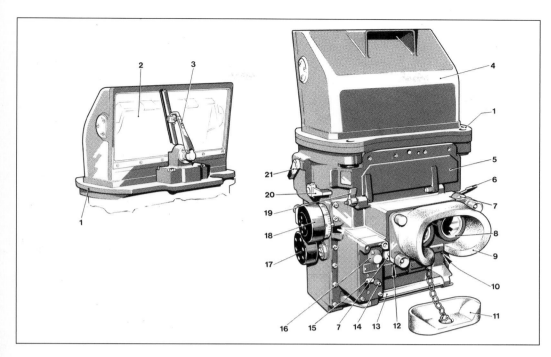

LEFT AND BELOW
Scorpion commander's sight, periscopic, AV, No 71.

As primarily a reconnaissance vehicle, CVR(T) is equipped with a range of optical devices for maximum observation under all conditions. The main commanders' sights for Scorpion and Scimitar are the No. 71 and No. 75 respectively. Manufactured by MEL Equipment Company, these binocular instruments offer ×1 and ×10 magnifications alternatively at the flick of a switch and give good visibility under poor conditions. For night operations, Scorpion and Scimitar incorporate the Rank Precision Industries SPAV L3A1 and L2A1 Image Intensification sights respectively. Each has a ×5.8 and ×1.6 high/low magnification for gunnery and surveillance. An electrically operated flash shutter (which functions from the gunfire circuit) protects the image intensifier tube from muzzle flash when firing.

The SPAV sight was a first-generation image-intensification (II) device as fitted to CVR(T) and Fox. It was effective for night-fighting, but this was very much dependent on the level of ambient light, so the brighter the night sky the better it performed. In April 1970, FVRDE conducted a trial to assess the capabilities of the prototype night sights fitted in Fox and Scorpion. It covered target acquisition of both static and moving targets against different backgrounds, together with

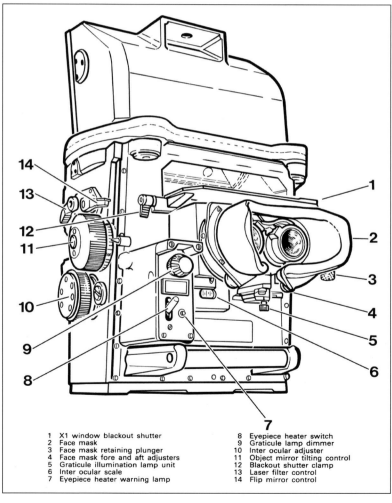

1	X1 window blackout shutter	8	Eyepiece heater switch
2	Face mask	9	Graticule lamp dimmer
3	Face mask retaining plunger	10	Inter ocular adjuster
4	Face mask fore and aft adjusters	11	Object mirror tilting control
5	Graticule illumination lamp unit	12	Blackout shutter clamp
6	Inter ocular scale	13	Laser filter control
7	Eyepiece heater warning lamp	14	Flip mirror control

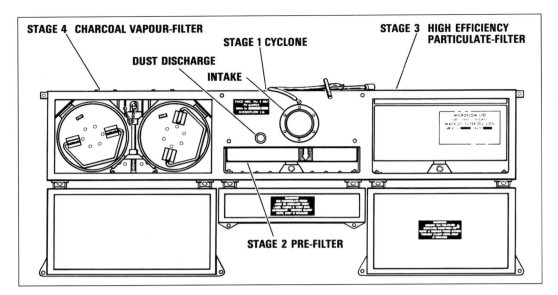

STAGE 4 CHARCOAL VAPOUR-FILTER
STAGE 1 CYCLONE
DUST DISCHARGE
INTAKE
STAGE 3 HIGH EFFICIENCY PARTICULATE-FILTER
STAGE 2 PRE-FILTER

firing of main and secondary armaments. It was concluded that, in general, the equipment operated satisfactorily and that, under suitable weather conditions, targets could be acquired at ranges up to 1,400m and engaged at ranges up to 1,200m.

Comprehensive vision is of the utmost importance in a reconnaissance vehicle and to this end the commander is provided with a periscope binocular sight ×10 with a unit power window in a rotating mount.

For night use, he has a passive night sight that is mounted on the right-hand side of the main armament. This sight has a large object lens with a magnification of ×5.8 (high) and ×1.6 (low) for gunnery and surveillance respectively using a conventional three-stage image intensifier.

Standard equipment on British Army Scorpions includes a Clansman radio communications system with the radios being installed in the turret bustle. A relatively large electrical capacity has been provided by incorporating two 100Ah batteries in the turret and two batteries in the hull. These are fed from a 140Amp 24V alternator. This arrangement gives a long silent watch capability that is so essential in a reconnaissance vehicle. Provision is made in the CVR(T) vehicles to protect the crew from radioactive fallout, biological and chemical weapons; commonly known as NBC protection. A four-stage NBC filtration pack is mounted at the rear of the fighting compartment of Scorpion and provides clean air under pressure. The filters and the complete unit can be removed for servicing through the external rear door. If NBC protection is deemed unnecessary, a further four rounds can be carried in its place.

Protection

Scorpion is the first all-aluminium AFV to be produced in quantity in the world but its principal form of protection is its compact size and agility, which ensure it is a difficult target to detect and engage. All the variants are of all-welded construction using an improved aluminium–zinc–magnesium AA7017 alloy, fabricated to the Alcan E74S specification, with rolled plate, extrusions, castings or forgings being used in construction as appropriate. The armour provides protection over the frontal arc against 14.5mm (0.59in) Armour-Piercing (AP) rounds and against 7.62mm (0.30in) AP elsewhere – the 14.5mm calibre being that of the standard Soviet AFV-mounted heavy machine gun. All-aspect protection is afforded against shell fragments from High Explosive (HE) 105mm rounds, either ground or air burst, at over 33yd (30m) distance. The hull configuration is designed to lessen mine blast and additional armour plate is welded to the floor of the driver's compartment to give him extra protection.

However, the innovative use of aluminium armour did present problems in subsequent

RIGHT The CVR(T) series was manufactured of aluminium–zinc–magnesium alloy fabricated by Alcan of Wolverhampton. However, the armour made by Sidal of Belgium was more prone to stress corrosion cracking (SCC). The remedial programmes to rectify the problem of SCC were lengthy and costly.

years when a condition known as stress corrosion cracking became apparent in the late 1970s. The effect was caused by variations in the microstructure of the armour plate during manufacture. At its worst, visible cracks appeared in the armour which did little to enhance the crews' faith in their vehicles. The problem was most serious in the gun mantlets of Scimitars, which were subsequently fabricated by alternative means. After extensive research at the Military Vehicles Experimental Establishment (formerly FVRDE) at Chertsey, a remedial programme codenamed Exercise Scorepole was initiated on 4 April 1978 in the UK and on 1 July 1978 in BAOR. A separate programme codenamed Exercise Maypole was undertaken to rectify the issue for foreign CVR(T) customers. These restored all vehicles to serviceable condition. Subsequently strict quality control in manufacture of the AA7017 alloy configured to the Military Vehicles Engineering Establishment's (MVEE)1318B specification, with further additional controls in fabricating, has virtually eliminated the problem.

Air portability

A fundamental requirement for CVR(T) was for all variants to be air portable by both helicopters and medium-lift transport aircraft such as the C-130 Hercules. In many respects this posed significant design limitations both in the overall dimensions and battle weight of the complete family. The General Staff Requirement demanded that

RIGHT CH-47D Chinook medium-lift helicopters transport underslung Spartan APCs during a training exercise on Salisbury Plain. Such a capability is a significant force multiplier on the modern battlefield.

53

Scorpion 03FD03 was married with a special Medium Stressed Platform (MSP) Mark 3A combined with extractor and delivery parachutes. The all-up weight (AUW) of the load on its platform was approximately 21,000lb. This weight required five 66ft Mark 3 parachutes for support. Even so, the Scorpion was only able to carry limited ammunition and fuel loads. Mud flaps and side skirts were removed, while other vulnerable fittings were stowed inside the vehicle. The trial showed that the Scorpion CVR(T) and MSP had to be the forward load in the aircraft. The airdrop must be undertaken at 1,200ft above ground level. Although the airdrop method proved to be feasible, it was never adopted operationally.

The tactical and strategic transport by RAF C-130 Hercules aircraft posed few problems. However, this was an expensive form of deployment, so was not undertaken lightly. Proving flights were made in support of ACE Mobile (Land) both to Norway and on the southern flank of NATO. In July 1974, CVR(T) Scorpions were first air-landed operationally by C-130 to Cyprus as reinforcements for the British garrison during the Turkish invasion of the island. A further operational deployment was made in October 1976 when a troop of Scorpions was flown to Belize to augment

any two of the vehicles be carried to a range of 1,000 miles and for one to be delivered by parachute airdrop on a special platform. By its very nature, the latter procedure was highly complex and, on occasions, fraught with hazard. The transport of CVR(T) by heavy- and medium-lift helicopters was relatively straightforward and was first proven by a US Marine Corps CH-53 in July 1973.

In May of the following year, a trial was undertaken by the Joint Air Transport Establishment to prove the airdrop method.

RIGHT O3FD03 came to grief in an abortive Air Landing operation in May 1973. After further trials, the British Army terminated the concept. The US Army refined the technique for the M-551 Sheridan with LAPES or Low Altitude Parachute Extraction System.

ABOVE AND LEFT In May 1973, Scorpion 03FD03 underwent airdropping trials at an all-up weight of 16,458lb for the basic vehicle plus CES at 15,148lb; II sight unit at 50lb; 40 rounds of 76mm at 665lb; 15 boxes of 7.62mm plus grenades etc., at 665lb and sundry stowage at 300lb. One of the Mark 3 parachutes failed to deploy properly with the unfortunate result seen opposite on page 54. Thereafter, Scorpion prototypes were used for parachute extraction trials on the basis that they were time-expired, but again with unpredictable results.

the resident British contingent and Harrier detachment in the face of Guatemalan provocation and the threat of invasion.

On 18 May 1982, II Squadron of the RAF Regiment was placed on alert to deploy a flight of CVR(T) to the Falkland Islands and, despite assembling at RAF Lyneham, the operation was cancelled at the last moment. Similarly, CVR(T)s were readied for deployment to Sierra Leone to support 1 PARA during Operation Palliser in the exact type of operation for which the Scorpion family was actually developed. Again, however, it never happened. Throughout the British Army's years of Peace Support Operations in the Balkans, CVR(T)s were airlifted to Bosnia as necessary although the majority went by sea. The CVR(T) was deployed operationally by RAF C-17 Globemaster to Macedonia at the

outset of Operation Agricola and the liberation of Kosovo in 1999. Further flights by C-17 and the massive Antonov An-225 Mryia strategic airlift aircraft transported CVR(T) Spartan Mark 2 AFVs directly to Camp Bastion in the Helmand Province of Afghanistan.

Water mobility

One of the novel features of the CVR(T) family was the ability of all variants to negotiate rivers and inland waterways by means of a folding, rubberised flotation screen around the top of the hull. With the screen erected, the vehicle propelled itself in water by using its tracks. During the 1960s, the General Staff deemed such a capability essential for all classes of AFVs since West Germany had many rivers running south to

RIGHT A fundamental design parameter for CVR(T) was an ability to negotiate inland waterways. A prototype Scorpion undergoes water crossing trials with the flotation screen erected at the Royal Engineers Wyke Regis Training Area near Weymouth. This CVR(T) is negotiating the tidal lagoon of Chesil Beach in almost perfect conditions with a gently sloping firm exit point: a situation unlikely to occur on operations.

north that would radically affect the conduct of armoured warfare in the face of an offensive by the Warsaw Pact member nations. The latter possessed many AFVs that were able to cross waterways with the minimum of preparation. The contemporary Soviet equivalent to CVR(T) was the PT-76 that incorporated hydrojets for propulsion in water and required no preparation beyond deploying a trim vane and engaging the bilge pumps. Accordingly, it was a true amphibious tank as its designation of Plavayushchiy Tank 76 or Floating Tank 76 affirms. Similarly, Soviet MBTs were able to negotiate many waterways by means of snorkel equipment with minimum preparation.

Such equipment was tested on the British Chieftain MBT but it was not adopted operationally while flotation screens were incorporated in such AFVs as late model Ferrets and the FV430 series. For CVR(T), the system was supposed to provide a water speed of 4mph (6.5kph) as against 6.4mph (10.2kph) for the PT-76. The reality was somewhat different as trials conducted at the Fording Trials Branch (FTB) at Instow in Devon in November 1970 revealed. It was found that water speed was rarely able to achieve any headway except with the engine running at 4,500rpm in fifth gear while steering was marginal. The turning circle in anything other than calm water was eccentric and steering

RIGHT The fully amphibious PT-76 was one of the principal Soviet reconnaissance AFVs at the time of the introduction of CVR(T). Accordingly, the L21 30mm Rarden cannon of Scimitar was designed specifically to defeat the PT-76 and its companion vehicles such as the BTR series of APCs. The PT-76 was also instrumental in the demise of Scorpion.

LEFT A Scorpion climbs out of a water tank with its flotation screen erected during a demonstration at Bovington. Even in such benign conditions one of the screen struts has become distorted, requiring time-consuming repairs for the screen to ever function again properly.

CENTRE Appliqué propeller units were developed to improve the manoeuvrability of CVR(T) during water crossing operations that were attached to the front drive sprockets.

response was too slow. This was exacerbated in any current greater than 2 knots, which also affected the vehicle's ability to exit from the water. Indeed, this proved to be the major problem since as soon as the tracks touched a riverbank, the driver was obliged to engage second gear to gain traction but any significant current could cause the vehicle to be swung around and the exit compromised.

It was apparent that propulsion by the vehicle's tracks was unsatisfactory so bolt-on or appliqué propeller units were developed that were attached to the drive sprockets. This equipment both increased water speed to 6mph (9.65kph) at the same time improving manoeuvrability. However, it took over 30 minutes to fit the propeller units that had to be carried in the echelon and brought forward when required. This of course compromised the whole concept of rapid crossing of waterways by CVR(T).

As late as 1978, experiments continued for self-extraction of CVR(T) from waterways and muddy banks by means of a hub winch attachment to the front sprocket wheels. Again, these had to be fitted before crossing a river but, of course, instead of the appliqué

LEFT Even with the appliqué propellers fitted, manoeuvrability in water was less than impressive and so a splashboard had to be added to maintain direction and the integrity of the flotation screen. With all this additional equipment, the concept of immediate water crossing by the vehicle crew alone was fatally flawed and the system was abandoned by the British Army but continued to be an option for foreign customers.

A series of photographs from a trials report show the capstan hub self-recovery device for CVR(T).

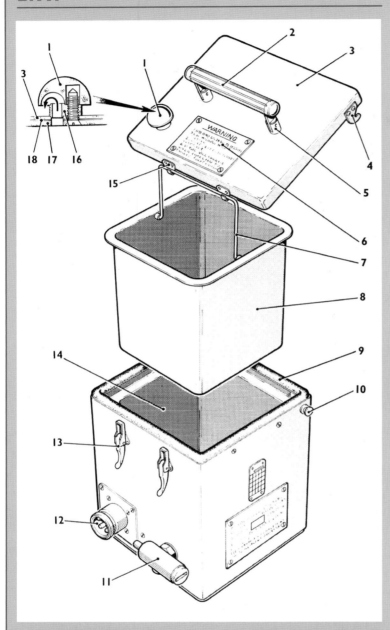

Possibly the most important item of equipment in any British Army AFV is the Electrothermal Engineering Ltd cooking and boiling vessel, known universally as the 'BV' or 'bivvi'. The boiling vessel is not only for making beverages such as tea, more tea and yet more tea, but also for frying eggs, bacon, sausages and other solid foods. It provides hot water for washing and shaving, as well as heating combat ration tins and pouches. Food and drinks can be prepared on the move and kept hot for up to four hours due to the efficient insulation. The BV can provide a gallon of boiling water or five cans of heated combat rations in 25 minutes. A fully functioning BV is an utter necessity in the British Army's prosecution of armoured warfare.

propellers, so propulsion in water was severely compromised. The crew were then obliged to drag an earth anchor to firm ground before the winch hubs could be engaged for recovery – an unsatisfactory procedure during an opposed crossing when under fire.

Eventually, the use of flotation screens within the British Army was abandoned and they were removed in the early 1980s. This followed the death of an FV432 driver when entering the River Weser at too steep an angle, causing the screen to collapse and the APC to sink. All told, the flotation screen was one of the most unpopular items associated with CVR(T) for their crews, so no one was displeased at its departure.

ABOVE AND BELOW All variants of CVR(T) were required to be amphibious by means of a flotation screen, as was CVR(W) Fox, as here, showing the limited vision of the drivers and the need for them to be directed by the vehicle commanders. Once the screens were removed in the early 1980s, the crews had far greater opportunity to add further stowage boxes and bins on their 'wagons': a win-win for all CVR(T) crew members.

CVR(T) variants

The original requirement for the replacement of the Ferret and Saladin armoured cars was a single multi-purpose reconnaissance vehicle capable of both direct fire support and the destruction of heavy armour at long range. Despite several significant projects, such as the Armoured Vehicle Reconnaissance, the concept proved elusive. That was further compromised by the necessity of the vehicle to be both air portable and amphibious. This led to the Lightweight High Mobility Tracked Family that embraced the many battlefield roles envisaged but lacked the full capability needed in general warfare. Even with the design and development of the Combat Vehicle Reconnaissance FV100 series well advanced, the possibility of combining both gun and missile armaments was investigated. Again this did not prove feasible because their width compromised the air portability requirement, so the roles were separated between the FV101 Scorpion Fire Support and the FV102 Striker Anti-Tank Guided Weapon Vehicle.

This demanded a different hull for Striker but with the same automotive, chassis and suspension components for maximum commonality. This allowed an expansion of the CVR(T) series with the FV103 Spartan APC and FV106 Samson ARV using the same hull as Striker. By a simple enlargement of this hull, a further two models were created with the FV104 Samaritan Armoured Ambulance and the FV105 Sultan Armoured Command Vehicle. Finally, a further version of Scorpion known as FV107 Scimitar was envisaged for close reconnaissance within mechanised infantry units armed with a 30mm cannon to destroy opposing APCs and Light Armour. This provided for a family of seven versions of CVR(T) as described in the following subsections.

FV102 Striker Anti-Tank Guided Weapon Vehicle

Striker is the first purpose-designed anti-tank guided weapon vehicle to be deployed with the British Army. The first production Striker was delivered in June 1975 and it entered service with the Royal Horse Artillery in BAOR in 1976.

Subsequently, the role of anti-tank artillery was transferred to the Royal Armoured Corps. The primary function of Striker is to destroy enemy armour at ranges out to 2.5 miles (4km) using hit-and-run tactics with its high agility and low profile, reducing the risk of detection. Although the 76mm HESH round of Scorpion can destroy opposing armour, Striker is the primary tank destroyer in the CVR(T) family.

Striker carries five British Aerospace Swingfire missiles in an armoured launcher bin at the rear of the hull. The launcher is raised to an angle of 35° by a hydraulic ram for firing. Once the operator has selected a target, a Swingfire missile is launched and he guides it on to the target using a thumb controller that produces guidance signals transmitted via a wire link dispensed from the rear of the missile. The Swingfire missile weighs 61.6lb (28kg) and is fitted with a High Explosive Anti-Tank (HEAT) warhead, capable of penetrating approximately 800mm of Rolled Homogeneous Armour (RHA): its performance against MBTs fitted with armour packages such as Explosive Reactive Armour (ERA) is significantly degraded.

Ordinarily, targets are engaged at long range by Striker from dead ground with only the sights and launcher bins visible, making the vehicle more difficult to locate and destroy. Once the five Swingfire missiles in the launcher bins have been fired, one of the crew members has to leave the vehicle to reload them with another five missiles, which are stowed under armour

ABOVE The FV102 Striker was originally issued to the Royal Artillery as here with Minden Battery, 12th Royal Artillery Regiment. Note the spent Swingfire guidance wires and missile containers beside the vehicle.

in the rear hull, giving a total of ten missiles carried. A remote sighting assembly allows the launching vehicle to adopt a hull-down, or concealed, firing position. Used by a single operator, the remote sight can be located up to 100m away from the vehicle. Striker has a battle weight of 18,400lb (8,346kg).

In early 1990, British Aerospace was awarded a £35 million contract from the MoD to upgrade the British Army Striker/Swingfire fleet over a five-year period. Much of the existing missile control and selection system was replaced by a new guidance and tracker system with an Automatic Command Line-of-Sight (ACLOS) capability. This greatly improved guidance accuracy with fewer demands on the operator. The Striker was withdrawn from service with the British Army in 2004.

FV103 Spartan armoured personnel carrier

Developed to GSOR 3385 as a replacement for the FV603 Saracen, the FV103 Spartan was designated as an Armoured Personnel Carrier or CVR(T) APC. Its primary role was to carry specialised teams undertaking particular tasks on the battlefield. The Spartan shares a similar hull configuration to Striker

ABOVE A Swingfire missile leaps from its launcher bin during early trials by BAC at Otterburn in 1973. Of particular note, this prototype Striker has two Bofors Lyran 71mm mortar tubes beside the driver's position to fire illuminating flares out to 1,500m. These were not fitted on production Strikers.

BELOW In its last operational commitment, the CVR(T) Striker proved highly effective in the few long-range engagements against Iraqi armour during Operation Telic in 2003. During the campaign, Striker was employed by the Household Cavalry Regiment and 1st The Queen's Dragoon Guards. Striker was withdrawn from service in 2004.

LEFT An FV102 Spartan APC DSL Bowman of the Royal Welsh Regiment comes ashore from an LCU during Exercise Runaground in October 2010. The Spartan has become the *de facto* 'battlefield taxi' of numerous British Army units.

but with seating for four soldiers in the rear compartment. These included support troops integral to armoured reconnaissance squadrons that acted as dismounted infantry to carry out patrols, provide close-in protection, conduct surveillance in conjunction with the crew as well as other tasks.

Spartan was employed by the Royal Engineers in armoured engineer and field squadrons for reconnaissance with bridging, breaching and assault elements during offensive and defensive operations. In the Royal Artillery, Spartan was the mobile platform for anti-aircraft Blowpipe and Javelin teams. In the infantry, Spartan was used by mechanised battalions to carry Mortar Fire Controllers coordinating fire support of 81mm mortars mounted in FV432 APCs as well as forward observers directing artillery fire. Indeed, all arms of service equipped with

BELOW After several days of driving through dust and mud in the field, a Spartan merges into the landscape as a Royal Engineers recce unit takes part in Exercise Uhlan Eagle 99 in Poland.

LEFT From the outset, the FV103 Spartan was designed to accept the Marconi ZB298 ground surveillance radar. Being a first-generation device, the ZB298 doppler radar could only detect moving objects and it took a skilled operator to be able to identify any potential target among the ground clutter. The system displayed both visual and audible signals of battlefield movement. The sound that was emitted was reminiscent of the character on a spring in the children's TV programme, *The Magic Roundabout,* and because of its ZB designation, the equipment was known to troops as Zebedee.

BELOW A prototype FV103 Spartan fitted with the later No 16 commander's cupola undergoes a stowage trial at FVRDE. It was originally intended to carry four troops in the back but there was only space for three and their personal equipment. Although the simplest design in the CVR(T) series, Spartan did not enter service with the British Army until 1978.

LEFT At the end of a serial during an FTX, the first priority is to have a brew after a Samaritan returns to the squadron hide on Salisbury Plain. The hamper above the Samaritan roof contains the vehicle CES and boxes of smoke grenades to allow all necessary medical supplies to be carried inside the vehicle.

BELOW The FV104 Samaritan was a major asset during the repeated UNHCR humanitarian aid convoys to the dispossessed peoples displaced by the bitter war in the Balkans. An ambulance was integral to all such convoys, codenamed Operation Cabinet, to provide immediate medical aid to all and sundry as with this Samaritan of B Squadron, The Light Dragoons.

Spartan use it extensively in a liaison role as the proverbial 'battlefield taxi' instead of Ferret.

As with all variants of CVR(T), Spartan is air portable and amphibious by means of a wading screen. It shares the same automotive performance and protection standards as the others to provide a highly versatile AFV that was procured in higher numbers than any other CVR(T) variant at 691 vehicles: more than twice as many as the next variant, Scimitar. Spartan can carry a ground surveillance radar such as the ZB298 and subsequently MSTAR, as well as night observation devices. Such devices consume high power loads, so battery life is critical – charging is possible with the engine running almost inaudibly at low speed to maintain silent watch.

FV104 Samaritan Armoured Ambulance

Samaritan is the armoured ambulance variant of the CVR(T) family and is designed primarily for casualty evacuation from forward battle areas. Using a hull similar to that of Sultan, the Samaritan has, in addition to the driver and medical orderly, accommodation for either four stretcher cases, two stretcher cases and three sitting cases or five sitting cases. In peacetime the rear of the Samaritan

is usually configured to carry four stretcher cases. These four are stowed in folding racks, two on each side of the vehicle, and with the racks folded away seats alongside either side of the vehicle become available for seated casualties. Standard equipment includes an NBC system mounted in the bustle on the rear door and extensive external stowage for medical supplies and stores. The Samaritan is also provided with an air-cooling system for the occupants' comfort. Medical supplies can

be carried on the top of the hull and in the rear of the vehicle. The variant has a battle weight of 19,100lb and is air portable by helicopter or transport aircraft. The first Samaritan was delivered to the British Army in May 1977.

FV105 Sultan Armoured Command Vehicle

The FV105 Sultan is an Armoured Command Vehicle employed in large numbers by the British Army as mobile control posts for commanders from squadron level upwards in virtually every formation on the battlefield. The Sultan has the same hull as Samaritan but is modified for use in the command post role. Sultan has a crew comprising driver, commander, radio operator and two or three 'watchkeepers' seated on the left side on the vehicle facing a map board on the right side. To increase the amount of working space, a

ABOVE The original concept for Samaritan featured a rounded top to the hull but changed to a flat slope as shown here before the hull side was extended vertically to give more internal space. The first Samaritan was delivered to the British Army in May 1977.

RIGHT With the orange tape and Maltese Cross indicating OPFOR or Opposing Forces, a Sultan command vehicle of 1st Royal Tank Regiment moves at speed to another tactical hide during an exercise on Salisbury Plain. Below the Chinese Eye, the vehicle is named 'Sir Percy Hobart' after the famed commander of the 79th Armoured Division during the Second World War.

LEFT AND ABOVE Analogue and digital – Sergeant Mark Webster RRF keeps a record of events with a lead pencil through the night as a 'watchkeeper' in the rear of a Sultan during an exercise in Poland in October 1999, while Lance Bombardier Pockett RA controls a Desert Hawk III UAV with an electronic pen during an FTX at BATUS in October 2015.

ABOVE Each Sultan command vehicle carries a folded fabric penthouse at the rear to create a larger working space when stationary or by combining with other Sultans, as seen here with Squadron Headquarters, A Squadron, The Queen's Dragoon Guards, during Operation Desert Sabre in February 1991.

RIGHT The original configuration of the 'high rise' CVR(T) variants, Sultan and Samaritan, featured sloping hull sides to the roof line. The panel on the hull side of this prototype Sultan gives access to the NBC equipment while the housing at the rear is an air-conditioning unit that was not fitted to production vehicles.

ABOVE Waiting for fuel in a 'replen line', a Samson ARV of the King's Royal Hussars displays the tools of its trade with the twin arms of the recovery spade at the rear and the central three-prong section on the hull side, with oil drip trays above to conform to German environmental laws.

tent can be erected at the rear of the vehicle. Due to the extensive array of communications equipment on board, the Sultan has a total of eight 12V batteries, while other members of the CVR(T) carry four.

FV106 Samson Armoured Recovery Vehicle

The FV106 Samson Armoured Recovery Vehicle (ARV) is an integral vehicle to support any formation using CVR(T). Samson can effect recovery of all members of the range as well as carry out front-line repairs in the field. With a crew of three or four, the vehicle is manned by the Royal Electrical and Mechanical Engineers (REME). Housed in the rear hull is a heavy-duty recovery winch driven from the main engine. The winch has a variable speed of up to 91m/min (300ft/min) on the 229m (750ft) of wire rope. Maximum pull,

RIGHT A Samson of A Squadron, 1st The Queen's Dragoon Guards takes to the desert of Al Fadhili soon after the arrival of A Squadron in Kuwait as the reconnaissance element of 7 Armoured Brigade, the Desert Rats.

with a 4:1 snatch block, is 14 tons. Samson's low ground pressure of 5.2lb/in^2 (35.85kN/m^2) facilitates the recovery and towing of both armoured and wheeled transport vehicles in terrain normally considered too difficult for heavier recovery vehicles. Samson was the last CVR(T) variant to enter service with the British Army, with the first deliveries taking place in 1978, as problems had persisted with the recovery winch.

ABOVE Flying the Latvian national flag, British troops demonstrate the capabilities of the Samson ARV following the sale of 123 CVR(T)s to the Latvian armed forces in 2014. These included Scimitar, Spartan, Sultan, Samaritan and Samson variants.

BELOW A Samson prototype is tested to the limit at the School of Electrical and Mechanical Engineers at Bordon in Hampshire. The first prototype of the Samson ARV was completed in 1973 with the first production vehicles being delivered in 1977; however, mechanical and reliability problems associated with the winch delayed its entry into full-time service. It was the last CVR(T) variant to be deployed with the British Army from 1978.

FV107 Scimitar 30mm Gun

While Scorpion undertakes medium reconnaissance for divisional formations out to a distance of 20 miles or more, the FV107 Scimitar is the close reconnaissance vehicle for their individual battle groups out to 3 miles. Scimitar has the same hull and turret as the Scorpion but is armed with an L21A1 30mm Rarden cannon in a different mantlet, with a coaxial L23A1 7.62mm machine gun. Both weapons have a depression of -10° and an elevation of +35° from the horizontal, the latter giving a useful deterrent effect against helicopters and low-flying aircraft – as was

demonstrated during the Falklands Campaign. The Rarden 30 is designed to fire all types of Oerlikon Buhrle 30mm ammunition, including Armour-Piercing Discarding Sabot (APDS) and High Explosive Incendiary HE/I rounds with a maximum range of 4km and 5km respectively. Ammunition stowage includes 165 rounds of 30mm, 3,000 rounds of 7.62mm and 16 smoke grenades over and above the 8 in the multi-barrel smoke dischargers mounted on the turret front face.

The L21A1 can defeat light AFVs and APCs out to 1,000m and beyond with considerable accuracy using APDS ammunition. When loaded with HE shell, it will deal effectively with soft targets such as men under light cover and trucks to a range of 2,000m. High accuracy has been achieved with light weight and low trunnion loading, the mechanism being housed within a compact light alloy casing, with a short inboard length of 43cm. Rapid single-shot fire ensures economy in ammunition expenditure while six rounds can be fired without reloading. Bursts of up to six rounds can be fired if desired. Empty shell cases are ejected out of the vehicle: this means that the turret is neither cluttered by empty cases nor affected by powder fumes, and the fighting efficiency of the crew is kept at peak even in continuous engagements.

LEFT The compact size of Scimitar makes it ideal as a close reconnaissance vehicle if not for its crew. The British Army has employed a basic camouflage scheme of black stripes over the green base colour for many years although it can be effective as shown by this Scimitar of B Squadron, The Blues and Royals on exercise on Salisbury Plain.

LEFT Prototype 00SP99 is shown to Scimitar production standard including the gunner's night sight. The first of three prototypes was delivered in July 1971 and Scimitar was accepted for service in June 1973. However, series delivery to the British Army was delayed due to a lack of Rarden 30mm guns and their spare parts.

Chapter Three

CVR(T) in service

—◉————————————

The Scorpion CVR(T) entered British Army service in 1972 with the other variants following during the course of the decade. CVR(T) was to prove its worth in many campaigns over the next 50 years and was held in high esteem by its crews, which is a fitting accolade for any AFV.

OPPOSITE A pair of Scimitars of 1st Royal Tank Regiment keeps close watch on proceedings during an Exercise Phantom Bugle on Salisbury Plain Training Area. The FV107 Scimitar was the final version of CVR(T) to be proposed but was the last to be retained as a gun platform in which role it has proved to be highly successful from close reconnaissance to peacekeeping duties.

Glory Hawk

In the early 1970s, industrial unrest was rife across the United Kingdom. This had a significant effect on the production rate of Scorpion and the other CVR(T) variants, particularly in the supply of components from subcontractors. The rate of inflation was rising alarmingly and government spending increasingly compromised. Defence spending was reduced in real terms in 1966, 1968 and 1969, the latter being a severe cut of 7%. By the end of the decade spending on defence had fallen to 4.65% of GDP. Scorpion was hurried into service in 1972 in order to forestall the possibility of cancellation in the expected cuts in the defence budget that occurred later in the year. Accordingly, several components, notably the gunner's image intensification night sight, were not fully developed before production began and others had not been tested to the usual thorough degree. As a result, several niggling problems arose in the early years but, with increasing User experience and a greater availability of spares, these were eventually overcome.

In all, some 400 Post Design Services modifications were applied to CVR(T) in the early years but nearly all were of a minor nature. With continued research by Alvis, most of these were rectified during a base overhaul modification programme codenamed

Exercise Bargepole, which began during 1975–76. The situation was exacerbated by the October War of 1973, after which the price of oil rose fourfold. Accordingly, the cost of fuel skyrocketed and the annual track mileage for CVR(T) was reduced by half to 1,000 miles per year. With the three-day week in 1974, the inflation rate escalated to 16%, then 25% in 1975. The unit cost of CVR(T) rose in consequence, as did the price of spares and ammunition. As a case in point, a 76mm HESH round cost £42 in 1974 but by 1976 was £72 – an increase of 71%, while a 30mm HE round rose from £9 to £18.20 – an increase of 102%. Furthermore, the British Army was heavily committed to Operation Banner: 27,000 British military personnel were sent to Northern Ireland with all units providing troops for the Troubles. All these aspects would have a significant effect on training and operational commitments in the coming years.

It was against this backdrop that the CVR(T) Scorpion entered service with the British Army. The first regiment to be issued with Scorpion was The Blues and Royals (Royal Horse Guards and 1st Dragoons), then stationed at Windsor in October 1972. They were followed by the 17th/21st Lancers in Northampton Barracks at Wolfenbuttel, West Germany, with deliveries in February, March, July and November of 1973. In late April 1973, the 14th/20th King's Hussars, deployed from Tidworth to Herford, West Germany, where the TQM's department received the first three Scorpions for evaluation and scaling. Conversion courses immediately began on Scorpion and, in July, Annual Firing took place at Hohne, followed by regimental training at Soltau in its usual summer dust bowl. In September, A and C Squadrons deployed to the Harz Mountains to join up with B Squadron of the 17th/21st Lancers to undertake Exercise Glory Hawk. Getting its name from the Lancers' regimental motto 'The Death or Glory Boys' and the hawk insignia of the King's Hussars, the exercise tested the fundamental role of the cavalry as reconnaissance and covering force in BAOR.

Lieutenant Colonel Arthur Douglas-Nugent, when he was commanding his regiment, the 17th/21st Lancers, recalls those days thus:

BELOW A Scorpion of the 17th/21st Lancers adopts the classic stance of a recce vehicle with the turret pointing towards the enemy as the commander scans the horizon while the driver is ready to move off at speed.

The 17/21st Lancers first took delivery of the Scorpion at Wolfenbuttel in 1973. There was great excitement when the first vehicles arrived to replace our ageing Saladins and Ferrets. Two squadrons were soon equipped and after a winter of individual training, took part on Exercise Glory Hawk, with the 14/20th Hussars, similarly equipped, on a fine area to the north of the Moselle. This was the first real test of the vehicle that performed marvellously well and there were very few breakdowns. The drivers really enjoyed themselves as they motored up and down the steep and wooded hillsides, going to places which their wheeled counterparts would never have achieved.

It took some time, however, for the full potential of the vehicle to be realised. Long experience of the wheeled Saladin had conditioned commanders to driving on roads and tracks. A more positive directive

had to be given to persuade them to take to the fields and to chance their arm across country. The damage done was negligible, as the track exerts less pressure than a man walking and so the whole of a vast area of farmland was available for manoeuvres. The Scorpion was shown off to the press during this exercise and at one stage a ballpoint pen was run over without damage. Another highlight of Exercise Glory Hawk was a trip around the German Grand Prix motor racing circuit, the Nürburgring. Scorpion performed with distinction, breaking the lap record for a tracked vehicle!

One drawback of the Scorpion was the lack of stowage space for the crew's personal kit. This was particularly difficult in the troop leader's vehicle, as for some reason young officers always seem to bring enormous suitcases on exercises. In the early days, the vehicles looked rather

ABOVE The Scorpions of the 14th/20th King's Royal Hussars and the 17th/21st Lancers churn up the dust of a recently harvested field at the conclusion of Exercise Glory Hawk in the Harz Mountains in October 1973.

LEFT During the course of Exercise Glory Hawk, one Scorpion of the 17th/21st Lancers was detached to give a demonstration of its capabilities to the West German defence minister. On its return, the Scorpion was passing the famous Nürburgring grand prix circuit where, on Sundays for the price of 7DM, members of the public can drive their private vehicles around the racetrack. The crew decided to put their Scorpion through its paces and despite the reservations of German officials it did no damage to the track.

like tinkers' carts with all the impedimenta tied onto the turret. Unofficial bins were tied on; welding being difficult owing to the aluminium construction. Finally, an official modification was introduced which put a large bin at the back and that went a long way to clear up the Christmas tree effect. Even so, the Scorpion, particularly with a full load of ammunition, has very little space for all the gear required by the crew. I remember too that spare parts were initially in rather short supply. We had some problems with the oil seals in the gearbox and replacements were very slow in coming. It was explained that the vehicle had been issued early to get it to regiments and that a risk had to be taken on spares. Also, until Ordnance had had User experience, they were not prepared

BELOW Following the conclusion of Exercise Glory Hawk, a race was organised between the Scorpions of the Hussars (left) and Lancers (right) at the Nürburgring racing circuit. In consideration of regimental rivalry, the race was declared a dead heat. These are early production Scorpions with three cup smoke dischargers, solid metal exhaust shroud and no blast guard on the front flotation screen. They also lack II gunners' sights with the aperture covered with a simple blanking plate that provided no armour protection at all.

to scale for spares. I am sure that this was a mistake, though we did benefit by getting the vehicle earlier than we would have done.

The annual pilgrimage to the gunnery ranges at Hohne went off well with fewer than the usual number of problems. Because the gun was similar to that of Saladin, little retraining was necessary. The vehicle handled extremely well and gave a creditable if not scintillating performance. The rather looping trajectory of the HESH round makes correct range estimation absolutely vital and at first many errors were made. A rangefinder would have been a most valuable addition. Equally, in the early days, vehicles were not equipped with an II night sight, so that observation and shooting at night were only possible using white light from another source.

Another excitement was the swimming of the River Weser at Ohr Park upstream from the famous old town of Hameln [Hamelin]. It was laid on with a fine organisation and plenty of preparation, but it must be admitted that it was not a great success. There was a 4-knot current running, and relying only on tracks for propulsion meant that forward movement was hard to achieve when exiting. The vehicle did however swim and the exercise was certainly valuable if not very convincing. I believe that the Scorpion was accepted into the family of the regiment quicker than any other vehicle. It went well from the start, was liked by all the soldiers who served in it and was ideally suited to the job of reconnaissance, which it was required to do. It was indeed a soldier's vehicle, the right one for the job.

One of Arthur Douglas-Nugent's young troop leaders was Lieutenant Robert McKenzie Johnston. He also recalls the first days of Scorpion in the Regiment:

One of first things you notice about Scorpion, especially after a career on tanks and Saladin, is its speed. There you are at the traffic lights, a large Mercedes beside you, and as the lights change you pull away together and stay together all the way down the road. It does something for the British image. But speed like this does lead to unexpected problems – like maps, for instance. There is not just the difficulty of map reading when little errors become enormous ones in seconds, but the difficulty of refolding a map as large as a tank sheet at 50mph on a bumpy track. Every move seemed to need three or four refolds during the course of it unless you were an origami expert. But the speed had compensations: mobility was improved considerably – not only was the Scorpion allowed into areas where no other tracked vehicles had been allowed, opening up new exercise possibilities, but it was also able to go where no other vehicle had been able to go before. We did an exercise early on called Lobster Quadrille, where our aim was to infiltrate behind the enemy. We achieved it by driving up a riverbed at night, a route the enemy had not anticipated anybody using. You could motor along at very low revs, making it very difficult for anyone to hear you, or to place you if they could hear the engine.

With these advantages there was also the sighting equipment. Together they meant that for the very first time we used the vehicle as the rule rather than the exception when in an OP [observation post], which was very much more

BELOW Scorpion's entry into service coincided with the introduction of the Weston Simfire Tank Gunnery and Tactical Training System that allowed realistic simulated tank vs tank engagements with real-time casualties inflicted by laser projector. The latter is seen above the 76mm gun barrel with laser detector units above the smoke dischargers and a flash/bang generator on the hull side. On the turret roof is the Simfire control unit.

comfortable for a start and much more practicable. There were other little things about the Scorpion that we all liked at once. It had a heater, it required very little routine servicing, it had a magic tool kit – sockets and ratchets, what a change from Saladin – it had an even more magic bivvi [BV or boiling vessel]. Of course there were ticks. Stowage was a big headache after the roominess of Chieftain and even Saladin. Big men felt wedged into it, and there just seemed to be no room at all for one's kit. We improvised, fitting jerrycan holders onto the back bin and leaving off things we hoped we wouldn't need. But when we were issued with five days' food and ammunition on one exercise, well, we just had to give some of it back.

Aluminium was a soft metal. Every time we hit anything, even gently, like a tree in a wood, the flotation screen came off. Was it 168 nuts and bolts? And it never went on

again easily, the chassis seemed to deform while you watched! And those engine decks! I think they are hinged now, but we used to have to undo the bolts and lift them off even for halt parades. Someone always managed to drop a corner on to the radiator and hole it. Firing the gun was quite an experience. Such platform rock that it was very difficult to maintain a point of aim. And bad luck on the commander who forgot to move his head away before the gunner shouted 'Firing now!', for the hard rubber eyepiece around his sight used to leave its mark on his face and the bridge of his nose. The first day's firing always brought its crop of inexperienced commanders who seemed to be wearing goggles permanently! We had to fire over the back decks to begin with. We were told it was to let the instructors stand on the engine decks behind us, but I believe it was because the blast from the gun blew the flotation screen out. Small details have changed on the modern Scorpion from those early days. Most of our first ticks have been solved, especially stowage. But those first impressions, the speed, mobility and adaptability of Scorpion, they will remain.

BAOR – watch on the Rhine

Space precludes any account of the role of CVR(T) in BAOR where the Scorpion family served for almost 50 years. The introduction of CVR(T) coincided with the Arab–Israeli War of October 1973 that reaffirmed the importance of armour on the battlefield despite the emergence of widespread ATGW. The concept of the flexible all-arms battle group was now paramount. This was now evident in the order of battle (ORBAT) of an armoured division in BAOR. It now comprised two armoured regiments with Chieftain MBTs; three mechanised infantry battalions with FV432 APCs, each consisting of four companies and operating MILAN (from the French *Missile d'infanterie léger antichar*) medium-range ATGW among other support weapons; an artillery group composed of two regiments of FV433 Abbot 105mm SPGs;

BELOW Dawn on the Inner German Border (IGB) where recce regiments conducted innumerable patrols over the years. The first two regiments to be equipped with Scimitar in BAOR were 1st The Queen's Dragoon Guards and the 13th/18th Royal Hussars. When first deployed to the IGB, the VOPOs and border guards came out in force to photograph the new vehicle. Thereafter the Scimitar appeared with a drainpipe on the Rarden to become a 120mm armed tank; the next day with a dustbin and dustbin lid as an air defence radar vehicle; the next with quadruple polo sticks as an SPAAG and so on with over a dozen variants of Scimitar. Each time the 'new' AFV was met with a barrage of photographers keen to record the enemy's latest AFV.

a Swingfire battery with FV438 long-range ATGW (later CVR(T) Striker); an air defence battery of shoulder-launched SAMs; and a medium battery of M-109 155mm guns. For reconnaissance, the division was allocated an armoured reconnaissance regiment comprising a Regimental Headquarters and two medium-range reconnaissance squadrons, each operating 16 Scorpions, as well as a close-range reconnaissance squadron of some 20 Scimitars; an Army Air Corps regiment with Gazelle utility and TOW-armed Lynx anti-tank helicopters; and last but not least an engineer regiment and logistics units.

Medium reconnaissance was conducted by armoured reconnaissance regiments under the direct control of formation headquarters, usually at corps or division level. The scope of operations varied widely and could be conducted anywhere in the area of operations within the limits imposed by the range of communications – approximately 20 miles. While armoured reconnaissance units were mobile, agile and possessed good communications, CVR(T) had limitations in respect of armour and firepower. Their function was enhanced by reconnaissance helicopters allocated in direct support. Close reconnaissance was the responsibility of the

reconnaissance troops and platoons organic to armoured regiments and mechanised infantry battalions. These tasks were undertaken by FV107 Scimitar once it entered service from 1974. Dismounted reconnaissance remained primarily an infantry responsibility, although armoured reconnaissance regiments had some capability with specialised troops mounted in FV103 Spartan. While BAOR remained the main theatre of operations for CVR(T), it was also employed extensively across the world from the Arctic Circle to the jungles of Belize in accordance with its original design specifications.

Exercise Hardfall – ACE Mobile Force (Land)

'From Stettin in the Baltic to Trieste in the Adriatic, an Iron Curtain has descended across the Continent. Behind that line lie all the capitals of the ancient states of Central and Eastern Europe. Warsaw, Berlin, Prague, Vienna, Budapest, Belgrade, Bucharest and Sofia, all these famous cities and the populations around them lie in what I must call the Soviet sphere, and all are subject in one form or another, not only to Soviet influence but to a very high and, in many cases, increasing

ABOVE A Swingfire ATGW missile is fired from a Striker of 171 (The Broken Wheel) Battery of 32nd Guided Weapons Regiment, Royal Artillery, during training on the ranges of Larkhill in September 1978. The anti-tank role reverted to the Royal Armoured Corps in 1984 and thereafter Strikers served in the Guided Weapons Troops of armoured reconnaissance regiments.

ABOVE The first deployment of Scorpion with AMF (L) occurred in February 1973 for the annual Exercise Hardfall in Norway. At the end of the month, A Squadron moved to the firing ranges at Hjerkinn at an altitude of 3,000ft and a temperature of –30ºC where it was necessary to keep all optics scrupulously clean to prevent them freezing over and adjust range estimation to compensate for icy ammunition rounds.

BELOW The remit of ACE Mobile Force (Land) extended from the Arctic sea to the Mediterranean. On its first deployment on the Southern Flank of NATO, AFVs of A Squadron, The Blues and Royals, conduct a patrol in the mountains of northern Greece on the Bulgarian border in June 1973 during Exercise Alexander Express. On this deployment, the AFVs were flown to Greece by C-130 Hercules and returned home by LSLs.

measure of control from Moscow.' In his famous speech at Westminster College in Fulton, Missouri, on 5 March 1946, Winston Churchill defined the beginning of the Cold War with his immortal phrase – the 'Iron Curtain'.

With the creation of the North Atlantic Treaty Organization (NATO) and the Warsaw Pact, the confrontation line dividing Europe extended even further from the Arctic Circle in Norway to the Turkish border with Bulgaria. In 1960, a brigade-sized formation with troops drawn from all NATO countries was created to act as a quick reaction force to be deployed at the express command of the NATO Supreme Commander. It formed part of Allied Command Europe (ACE) with headquarters at SHAPE in Casteau, Belgium. It was designated ACE Mobile Force (Land) or AMF-L. Among the British armed forces contribution was the ground reconnaissance unit working in conjunction with the Harrier Force.

Originally armed with Ferret armoured cars, the reconnaissance unit was manned by the cavalry on detachment from their parent regiment for up to five months a year and for up to four years at a time to maintain their expertise in this specialised role. Areas for deployments included Norway, Denmark, Turkey and Italy at Trieste on the Yugoslav border – as Churchill's

Iron Curtain speech declaimed. For the rest of the year, troops trained for their next deployment and also took part in regimental training activities and duties. The very first six Scorpions issued to the British Army were part of the AMF-L squadron of The Blues and Royals in October 1972. The Scorpions of A Squadron were deployed to Norway that winter to undertake Exercise Hardfall within the Arctic Circle in what the squadron commander called '. . . the annual quest by the British contingent for the foulest possible conditions in which to carry out Arctic training. . . . The efforts of the British soldier on skis have for years provided the Norwegian populace with a never-ending source of free amusement.'

In the following year, A Squadron exchanged the bitter cold of Norway for the summer sunshine of Greece for Exercise Alexander Express during an AMF-L deployment on the southern flank of NATO. In November 1973, A Squadron was in Denmark to conduct Exercise Absalom Express and then returned to Norway for another Exercise Hardfall where the temperature dropped to -38ºC. In such conditions operating the Scorpion became difficult because the roads were covered in sheet ice and therefore the vehicle was prone to skidding and sliding into verges and ditches. When driving in snow deeper than 18in the Scorpion tended to 'belly' and lose traction. A Squadron continued in their AMF-L role until 1975 when The Blues and Royals converted to Chieftain MBTs as an armoured regiment in BAOR.

Thereafter, C Squadron The Life Guards assumed the task and it grew in importance as the only armoured element within AMF-L. During the winter deployment of 1975, training was undertaken as usual at Rinnliret and firing practice at the Jherkin ranges. Following Exercise Hardfall, the squadron was to conduct an exercise with the Norwegian Army near Narvik. Ordinarily, the squadron would have moved by sea in a Landing Ship Logistics (LSL) but it was decided to make the journey of 580 miles overland. At 0530 hours on 12 March, the squadron headed north in a snowstorm supported by a Forward Repair Team from 9 Field Workshops, two RCT petrol bowsers, two Army Air Corps

ABOVE An Army Air Corps Gazelle helicopter of the Force Reconnaissance Unit hovers behind a Scimitar of C Squadron, The Life Guards, during Exercise Hardfall in February 1977 with Lance Corporal of Horse Pace and Lance Corporal O'Connor in the turret. Typical of CVR(T) in Norway, the rubber pads of the track blocks of this Scimitar have had metal studs injected into them by high-pressure air guns to improve traction on ice.

BELOW The crew of a Scorpion of C Squadron, The Life Guards, cover their 'wagon' with a camouflage net during Exercise Atlas Express during Hardfall 1976. It was one of the coldest winters in Norway for 20 years with some of the heaviest snow falls as well: a truly testing environment for men and machines.

Gazelle helicopters and a Norwegian liaison officer. With temperatures ranging from -15°C to +15°C, the roads varied from metalled to graded soil with a covering of ice and snow. There were extensive stretches of narrow, winding mountain roads with long slippery gradients. Two high passes were traversed and two civilian ferries were used to cross fjords. The squadron took five days to complete the journey passing through some of the wildest and most beautiful scenery in Norway, arriving at Narvik on schedule and ready to participate in Exercise Cold Winter with the Norwegian Army. Problems continued when snow compacted between the idler or sprocket wheels causing the tracks to shed. Thereafter, the crew was left with the dismal task of recovery in the bitter cold. A team from MVEE joined Exercise Hardfall in 1979 to address the situation. New perforated idler and sprocket wheels were developed to alleviate the problem. The next regiment to take on the assignment to AMF-L was the 17th/21st Lancers.

With the widespread issue of FV107 Scimitar, it served in the reconnaissance troops of mechanised infantry battalions and with an RAC troop attached to standard infantry units committed to AMF-L. In August 1982, 15 Troop 4th Royal Tank Regiment (3 Troop D Squadron) returned from BAOR to the UK, to undertake such a role as close reconnaissance troop. After taking over their Scimitars and preparing them for the rigours of the Arctic, the troop moved to Southampton Docks where it boarded the SS *Dana Ventura* and sailed for Norway. The troop leader, Captain Phillip Skinner, takes up the account of the RTR deployment:

A week's intensive training in survival and cross-country ski techniques immediately began. The Norwegian Army officer attached to the company assisted our small nucleus of seasoned instructors. The confidence of living in snow acquired by us all, we were able then to concentrate on working up for the battalion training exercises with our vehicles. Sadly, CVR(T) has a severely limited cross-country performance in snow and for the winter

months it is effectively confined to the roads and 'Volvo tracks' [tracks of compressed snow that were created by Snow Trac and Bv202/206 all-terrain vehicles to aid the mobility of CVR(T)]. The lack of perforated sprockets and idlers – which had only just been issued for the vehicles – meant that the danger of throwing a track was ever-present even when executing the simplest of off-road manoeuvres and as a consequence our recce role was inevitably severely limited. Used, as we were, to a highly mobile role in Denmark and BAOR, we had to content ourselves with acting in the advance as fire support vehicles – a less demanding but vitally important role for which Scimitar, fitted with a Rarden gun of outstanding accuracy, range and a high rate of fire, is well suited. Furthermore, the vehicle optics were superb in Norway's dry atmosphere and II sights proved to be of much benefit to a dismounted infantry battalion sited in defence.

In addition to OP and close support work, the troop was extensively involved in route clearance, security and marking tasks, rear area security and, even in extremis, troop-carrying roles. Our engine decks were always highly sought after by the hapless infantry wherever we went – offering them an opportunity to dry out their sleeping bags, equipment and thaw out their frozen feet. With the phase in Southern Norway completed, the troop drove back to the port of Granvin at the beginning of March to sail north to participate in Exercise Cold Winter. Immensely important politically, it is a co-ordinated exercise featuring US and Canadian Airborne and Marines, elements of Brigade North, Norwegian Army and 3 Commando Brigade and is set in a secluded valley south of Narvik.

In 1986, the role of armoured reconnaissance with AMF-L was taken over by D Squadron of the 13th/18th Royal Hussars (Queen Mary's Own) by which time all variants of CVR(T) were in service. The squadron comprised 115 all-ranks, with four Sabre troops, a guided weapons troop, a support troop, a headquarters troop and enlarged

administrative and fitters troops. A Sabre troop was equipped with two Scorpions and two Scimitars while the GW troop had four Strikers. The other troops included Spartans, Sultans, Samaritan and a Samson together with several vital Hagglund Bv206 all-terrain vehicles. During their time in Norway, the 13th/18th Royal Hussars also devised a Scorpion snow plough for clearing roads and tracks. In 1991, 1st The Queen's Dragoon Guards assumed the role and so it rotated among the RAC regiments until AMF-L was disbanded in 2002.

Operation Trustee – the Boeing Patrol

With the rise of terrorism in the UK in the 1970s, London's principal airport of Heathrow was deemed to be a potential target for terrorists including Palestinians and the Irish Republican Army (IRA). The first IRA outrage occurred on 22 February 1972 with the bombing near the officers' mess of the 16th Parachute Brigade at Aldershot Barracks, killing 6 civilians, including female cleaning staff and an army padre, while 19 others were injured. There followed a dismal litany of Provisional IRA (PIRA) bombings across mainland Britain for the next 40 years. In January 1974, The Blues and Royals were tasked with supporting the Metropolitan Police for public security at Heathrow Airport with

ABOVE A Grenadier Guardsman patrols 'airside' with a Scorpion of C Squadron, The Blues and Royals, during an Operation Trustee deployment to Heathrow on 10 February 1982. (HCRM)

BELOW The deployment of troops to Heathrow Airport became routine as the threat of international terrorism grew over the years in what became known to old hands as 'The Boeing Patrol'. The last major occasion was on 11 February 2003 when AFVs of the Household Cavalry Regiment and some 400 troops came to the aid of the civil power during Operation Flak. (HCRM)

both Scorpions and Ferret armoured cars drawn from B Squadron under the designation of Operation Trustee. It was to become a recurring deployment over the forthcoming years.

On 9 March 1994, the PIRA fired five Mark 6 improvised mortar bombs from the car park of the Forte Excelsior Hotel on to Heathrow Airport's northern runway some 500m away. On the following day, Queen Elizabeth II was scheduled to land there on an RAF flight. It was the first of three mortar attacks on the airport in the space of five days. Other mortar bombs were fired from buried launch tubes but fortunately none of the 12 rounds exploded and damage was minimal. Tragically, this was not the case on 20 July 1982 when a PIRA improvised explosive device detonated in Hyde Park just as an Honour Guard of The Blues and Royals was passing. Four soldiers and seven horses were killed.

Following the Good Friday Agreement of 1998, the IRA threat diminished but that of Al-Qaeda soon came to the fore. Subsequently codenamed Operation Flak instead of Trustee, A and B Squadrons The Life Guards, together with C Squadron The Blues and Royals,

deployed to Heathrow Airport on 11 February 2003 as part of 450 troops and 1,000 extra police officers to boost security against the menace of suicide bombers and surface-to-air missiles. At the same time, D Squadron The Blues and Royals deployed to Kuwait to take part in Operation Telic.

Cyprus 1974 – the Turkish invasion

On 20 July 1974, Turkish troops landed in northern Cyprus near the port of Kyrenia and immediately advanced southwards to the capital Nicosia. On the previous day at 0430 hours, Regimental Headquarters (RHQ) and A Squadron, 16th/5th The Queen's Royal Lancers, were placed on 24 hours' alert to deploy to Cyprus. Equipped with CVR(T) Scorpion, A Squadron were flown by Hercules C-130 to RAF Akrotiri, with refuelling in Malta, together with RHQ where they were to form a composite armoured regiment, since B Squadron 16th/5th and C Squadron 4th/7th Dragoon Guards were already on the island as the resident armour contingent. Having been told to get the

troops to Cyprus in the shortest possible time, the RAF abandoned any semblance of tactical loading by trying to embark Light Aid Detachment (LAD) 4-tonners carrying spare parts first with RHQ vehicles way down the queue. On arrival at Akrotiri, the situation was chaotic to say the least with orders flowing from the Commander British Forces Near East, General Officer Commanding (GOC) Near East Land Forces, GOC British Forces Cyprus and the Commander UNFICYP. For the most spurious reasons, it was deemed to be 'politically unacceptable' for 'aluminium tanks' to operate on Cypriot soil, so the Scorpions were re-embarked on C-130s and flown to Pergamos Camp at the Sovereign Base Area Dhekelia, which the Turks had no intention of attacking. There the CVR(T) were confined to patrolling the base perimeter as the fighting raged elsewhere.

Accordingly, all the heavy lifting devolved to B Squadron, 16th/5th, in their Saladin and Ferret armoured cars to evacuate and escort to safety all the British civilians and service families dotted around the war zone to the Sovereign Base Areas. Despite their underemployment, further Scorpions of B Squadron, The Blues and

ABOVE A Scorpion of B Squadron, 16th/5th The Queen's Royal Lancers, drives out of a C-130 Hercules at Pergamos Camp during the Turkish invasion of Cyprus in 1974.

Royals, were despatched to Cyprus on 21 July. Again the RAF caused consternation with their loading plans as The Blues and Royals Journal recounts:

The fly-out went well enough, though our friendly local airways developed the irksome habit of putting Scorpions on one aeroplane and their crews on another. Inevitably one or the other plane broke down and the echelon vehicles were shut out for a couple of days, along with all those vital mechanical curiosities, which tended to be tiresome. But mostly it was fairly painless, thank goodness, because at the far end we motored off the aeroplanes straight to the ammunition compound and then out on patrol under command of 19 Airportable Brigade.

By now the value of CVR(T) was realised by the infantry-orientated high command and they were increasingly employed in the war zone with the Saladins operating up to Nicosia and the Scorpions around SBA Dhekelia and RAF Akrotiri. However, there was one incident of note when a Turkish M-47 approached a roadblock manned by 3 Troop, A Squadron, and spluttered to a halt having run out of petrol. It had also run out of main armament ammunition, the secondary armament was jammed, the radios did not work and the tank commander had no map or compass. This did not constitute any formidable threat, which could not be said of 'grape sickness' suffered by many crews. With no harvest in progress, the abundance of low-hanging grapes was too much of a temptation in the oppressive summer heat causing serious stomach upsets, let alone the copious quantities of Keo beer and brandy. Following a fragile ceasefire, the CVR(T)s were returned to the UK by sea.

BELOW Scorpions of A Squadron, The Blues and Royals, undertake a patrol along the road from Dhekelia to Famagusta during the evacuation of service families and British citizens to safety at the Sovereign Base Areas.

RIGHT The Scorpions of C Squadron, The Life Guards, were flown to Belize in C-130 Hercules transport aircraft with a refuelling stopover at Gander in Newfoundland.

BELOW Corporal of Horse Whyte of C Squadron, The Life Guards, conducts a patrol with Scorpion in July 1977 somewhere 'up country' in Belize where the writ of law was minimal. Accordingly, the CVR(T) undertook many important tasks in support of the Belize authorities such as interdicting drug runners and smugglers, as well as providing medical aid and succour to the native population in the interior.

Belize – the jungle confrontation

As a former colony, British Honduras gained its independence on 21 September 1981 to become Belize. For many decades, the neighbouring country of Guatemala had claimed much of its territory. Confrontation along the border continued for many years until Guatemala descended into civil war in 1975, whereupon Britain reinforced its resident infantry battalion with No 1417 Flight of six Harrier GR1 VTOL jets. Subsequently known as HarDet or Harrier Detachment Belize, the RAF flight and garrison were further reinforced with a ground protection force of a troop of Scorpions of B Squadron, The Life Guards, that were deployed by RAF C-130 Hercules transport aircraft in October 1976. Given the appalling road system in Belize, the CVR(T) contingent was soon supported by a REME Samson ARV once it entered service. The British Forces Belize, subsequently the British Army Training Support Unit Belize or BATSUB, were provided by the Belizean government with 500 square miles of secondary jungle terrain to allow visiting British Army units to undertake jungle warfare training.

Similarly, the Armoured Reconnaissance Troop was manned by personnel from cavalry regiments in the UK or BAOR on a six-month secondment. As a posting to the tropics, Belize certainly lived up to the expectations of army recruiting posters from the essential Belikin beer to the delights of La Casa Rosa. The next troop to serve in Belize was drawn from C Squadron, The Life Guards, under the command of Lieutenant C.B. Oldfield, who immediately declared himself to be Director Royal Armoured Corps or DRAC South Pacific that indicated an eccentric knowledge of geography. They were replaced by the Royal Scots Dragoon Guards and, like the AMF-L detachment, elements from other cavalry regiments followed year by year.

The primary role of the armoured reconnaissance troop was to 'show the flag' across the length and breadth of the country, particularly in those areas where the Belizean police did not hold sway, mainly because of their paucity of cross-country vehicles. Similarly, the CVR(T)s were transported to an area of operations by locally contracted low-loaders, despite the troop having an unlimited mileage allowance unlike in the UK or BAOR. Nevertheless, the demanding tropical climate, harsh terrain and primitive road system took a severe toll on the serviceability of the CVR(T) that was addressed by regular overhauls at the BATSUB workshops where all current modifications and updates were also implemented.

Yet the real purpose of the CVR(T) was to provide British forces in Belize with fire support in any confrontation with the 'Guats' as they were known in the contemporary vernacular. Tension along the border waxed and waned depending on the internal political situation in Guatemala. The Guatemalan armed forces had only 12 M-41 Walker Bulldog light tanks from the Korean War period, together with a number of M-113 APCs that could conceivably form a mobile striking force. Neither AFV posed a significant threat to the CRV(T)s as the Scorpions' 76mm armament firing HESH rounds was more than a match for them, while at the same time supporting infantry in both direct or indirect fire modes in the event of an incursion into

Belize. As it turned out, it was never put to the test and Belize was always a popular posting for CVR(T) crews despite the snakes, spiders and vexatious insects.

BATUS – the Salamander enemy

Following the loss of Libya as an armoured formation training area after the *coup d'état* by Colonel Gaddafi, the British Army entered into an agreement in 1972 with the Canadian government to lease some 1,000 square miles of rolling prairie in Alberta that became the British Army Training Unit Suffield (BATUS). Since then generations of armoured and mechanised infantry units have conducted some of the most realistic field training exercises (FTX) possible, complete with live ammunition firing of all calibres of weapons. As laser-based training aids such as SIMFIRE, SIMFICS and TES became more sophisticated, FTXs increased in pace and complexity against an OPFOR (or Opposing Force) employing standard Soviet doctrine and tactics. Depending on the period, a typical Exercise Medicine Man lasted some 30 days that was broken down into special-to-arms

ABOVE The Salamander was a Scorpion modified to resemble a Soviet MBT, such as the T-80, by adding empty fuel drums at the rear and a plastic pipe as a larger main armament as well as rubber side skirts. These Salamanders prowl the prairie as OPFOR to engage the armour of Battle Groups undertaking training at BATUS.

BELOW Among several CVR(T) conversions to simulate Soviet equipment at BATUS, these Spartans have simple wooden panels to represent the MTU-55 bridge-layer together with serrated metal panels at the front to mimic mine ploughs.

training, be it Challenger or Warrior; combined arms training with tanks, IFVs, sappers, gunners, aviation and so on; and finally a TESEX or Tactical Engagement Simulation Exercise against the OPFOR contingent: TESEX being the grand finale of the whole deployment.

Originally, OPFOR was equipped with standard CVR(T) Scorpions fitted with

SIMFICS, but over time the vehicles were provided with VISMODs (visual modifications) to make them appear to be specific Soviet AFVs such as T-80 MBTs or BMP IFVs. When the Spartan MCTs were withdrawn from service they were converted into an advanced OPFOR vehicle named Sturgeon, to continue the Russian theme, equipped with the latest electronic devices for targeting. Similarly,

the Scorpion was also altered and became known as Salamander since presumably it can change its appearance. However, neither Salamander nor Sturgeon had up-to-date night-fighting equipment, so they have been superseded by BGTI Scimitars with only limited VISMODs but able to conduct operations 24 hours a day against the five different battle groups that train at BATUS each year.

ABOVE Salamanders and Sturgeons of OPFOR replenish between serials during an FTX at BATUS in 1999. The OPFOR vehicles feature a distinctive three-colour camouflage scheme. Initially, the algorithm in the fire control systems of Salamander and Sturgeon was overly advantageous to OPFOR, resulting in too many 'defeats' for the battle groups on exercise so it was subsequently modified in the interests of fairness.

LEFT The Salamanders and Sturgeons have been superseded by standard BGTI Scimitars with limited VISMODs to allow 24-hour exercises for more realistic training. Of interest, the leading vehicle was previously an RAF EOD Scimitar.

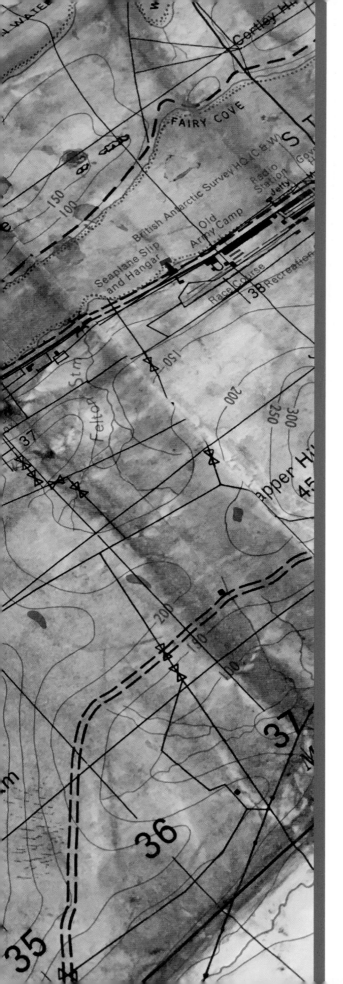

Chapter Four

CVR(T) in combat – the Falklands Conflict, 1982

The CVR(T) first saw combat during the Falklands Conflict of 1982 to restore British sovereignty following the Argentine invasion. Eight Scorpions and Scimitars of The Blues and Royals made a significant contribution to the land campaign out of all proportion to their number, providing vital fire support to the infantry battalions in the night battles for the hills overlooking the final objective, the capital, Stanley.

OPPOSITE This oil stained map was carried by a CVR(T) throughout the Falklands Conflict and shows the location of the final hill battles before the capture of Stanley. The map is currently on display at the Household Cavalry Regiment at Combermere Barracks in Windsor.

Operation Corporate

On 2 April 1982, Argentinian armed forces invaded the Falkland Islands – British sovereign territory. The small garrison of Royal Marines was overwhelmed and obliged to surrender after a stout defence lasting some four hours. The Argentine military dictatorship of President Leopoldo Galtieri declared the islands to be known henceforth as Las Malvinas and considered an integral part of Argentina. On the following day, the British government announced the despatch of a naval Task Force to the South Atlantic under Operation Corporate. The Task Force comprised more than 100 ships with over 28,000 personnel, including 3 Commando Brigade and 5 Infantry Brigade. Among the troops was a small contingent of CVR(T) vehicles of The Blues and Royals (RHG/D).

Based at Combermere Barracks in Windsor, The Blues and Royals were widely dispersed when the call to action came. A Squadron was in Cyprus and C on block leave with only B still at Windsor. Furthermore, half of B Squadron was on Easter leave, while squadron headquarters and two troops were preparing for an exercise on Salisbury Plain. On 4 April, the commanding officer, Colonel James Hamilton-Russell, was instructed to

ABOVE All the CVR(T) vehicles were transported southwards to Ascension Island aboard the MV *Elk*. They were accompanied by Corporal of Horse Stu Thomson, Lance Corporals Martin Mitchel and Lewis REME to undertake essential maintenance such as battery charging. Cross-decking to HMS *Fearless* was carried out on arrival at Ascension, with the vehicles from MV *Elk* and crews from SS *Canberra*.

RIGHT Despite the high command's reluctance to allow the CVR(T) to come ashore, it was essential to allow the Scorpions and Scimitars to boresight their main armaments and practise with the newly issued 30mm APDS round. Within short order, the Scimitars were hitting five-gallon oil drums at 1,500yd with regular precision.

RIGHT On the firing ranges near Wideawake Airfield on Ascension Island, 4 Troop engages targets, mainly old airfield equipment and fuel tankers, with Two Three Alpha waiting to the rear. Firing was undertaken in a two-vehicle serial with one Scorpion and one Scimitar working in mutual support. As Ascension Island is mostly volcanic soil, grass fires did not interrupt gunnery.

provide two reconnaissance troops, each with two Scorpions and two Scimitars as well as a REME Light Aid Detachment with a Samson recovery vehicle. The group was to be ready for embarkation at Southampton in two days' time. The constraints of availability reduced the choice to 3 Troop commanded by Lieutenant Lord Robin Innes-Ker and 4 Troop by Lieutenant Mark Coreth. As the senior subaltern, Lieutenant Coreth flew by helicopter to Plymouth for orders on 5 April but on his return to Windsor 'we found that even the paymaster had burned the midnight oil and kindly produced our mess bills before our departure!'.

The nine CVR(T) vehicles together with a maintenance party were loaded aboard the MV *Elk* on 6 April and the other crew members sailed from Southampton on the SS *Canberra* three days later on Good Friday.

The ship stopped at the British dependency of Ascension Island on 20 April. There the CVR(T) were unloaded and the crews were able to practise gunnery on Wideawake ranges despite some resistance from high command. The priority was to boresight their main armaments since this had not been done since the previous annual firing in November, as well as testing the new APDS round. A further trial was conducted on the feasibility of firing from the bows of landing craft. This proved possible

RIGHT Royal Marines practise their landing craft drills loading via scramble nets from HMS *Fearless* as a Scorpion and Scimitar wait in the bow of an LCU. In the case of an opposed landing, the CVR(T) were to deliver fire support with the Scorpion providing area fire and the Scimitar suppressive automatic cannon fire. Note the Scimitar is slightly behind the Scorpion so that the latter's gun blast does not affect the former's sighting.

BELOW Operation Sutton begins with landing craft of HMS *Fearless* and HMS *Intrepid* ploughing towards the shoreline of Port San Carlos, Ajax Bay and San Carlos at dawn on 21 May 1982. At 0500 hours, 3 Troop set off with 40 Commando for San Carlos Settlement while 4 Troop landed at Port San Carlos with 3 PARA.

if only as suppressive fire. Thereafter, the CVR(T) and crews were loaded on the assault ship HMS *Fearless* before sailing for the South Atlantic on 10 May.

Ten days later, HMS *Fearless* entered the Total Exclusion Zone encircling the Falkland Islands. En route, the vehicles were prepared for wading should the need arise. On 21 May, HMS *Fearless* dropped anchor in San Carlos Water at 0400 hours. Some delay ensued when the rear doors of the landing platform dock failed to open but this was soon rectified. With the CVR(T) and

men of 3rd Battalion, The Parachute Regiment (3 PARA), waiting in the darkness of the dock, the commander of Callsign Two Four Alpha of 4 Troop remembered that it was the birthday of his gunner, Trooper Mick Flynn. As the doors opened and the landing craft surged forward, the strains of 'Happy Birthday' could be heard as the CVR(T) crews and Paras sang lustily to mark the event.

Fortunately, the landing was unopposed with 3 Troop supporting 40 Commando, Royal Marines, on Blue Beach at San Carlos Settlement with Lance Corporal of Horse Fisher leading while 4 Troop came ashore with 3 PARA on Green Beach at Port San Carlos. Initially, their tasks on the beachhead were to provide fire support for the battalions clearing the area and then to occupy defensive observation positions on the surrounding hills.

Lieutenant Coreth recalled:

I sent Corporal of Horse Stretton and Lance Corporal of Horse Ward up to the aptly named Windy Gap to help protect the north-east flank. The air raids began and became a feature of daily life. By day we shot at aircraft which we enjoyed and by night we froze. Two days later I replaced Corporal of Horse Stretton at Windy Gap. On the way there we proved our point for the first

of many times. The experts had said that [CVR(T)] could not move on the Falklands terrain, we said they could. On the way we found a tractor up to its axles in a bog. Using our incredible kinetic energy rope we catapulted him out with the greatest of ease; all this with [CVR(T)] on a thin film of peat with almost liquid bog beneath.

Herein lay a fundamental failure of the high command to appreciate the capabilities of CVR(T). With its ground pressure that was less than a walking man and especially of a heavily laden infantryman in the Falkland Islands, CVR(T) was capable of negotiating virtually all the terrain encountered during the campaign. This misunderstanding manifested itself during the Battle of Goose Green when 2 PARA launched their assault without the provision of adequate fire support against an entrenched regiment-sized formation. At the outset of the battle there was naval gunfire support from HMS *Arrow* during the hours of darkness and in daylight, just three 105mm Light Guns of 8 Battery, 29 Commando Regiment, RA, as well as two 81mm mortars and three MILAN ATGM (Anti-Tank Guided Missile) launchers. Mortar ammunition ran out at a critical time and scheduled close air support was compromised by bad weather with just three sorties against

Argentine anti-aircraft guns, resulting in the loss of a Harrier GR3 and its pilot. It is ironic that the Scorpion CVR(T) was originally designed as a fire support vehicle for airborne and air-landed forces. At Goose Green the Scorpion was sorely missed. Nevertheless, through sheer determination and professionalism 2 PARA prevailed and the battle was won.

Back at the beachhead the CVR(T)s were dug in to increase protection against air attack. The first week was a time of frustration as the priority was to land supplies from the vulnerable shipping in San Carlos Water that was subject to constant air attack. On shore the main problem for the troops was the cold and wet as well as the frustration of inaction and at the ghastly spectacle of ships being bombed to destruction.

For The Blues and Royals irritation was compounded by the lack of fuel to run their engines and thus achieve a measure of warmth. The Royal Navy has a considerable antipathy towards petroleum spirit on board ships because of the fire hazard. Accordingly, as little as possible is carried and HMS *Fearless* would normally only have sufficient for its Centurion Beach Armoured Recovery Vehicle and certain generators. Thus, petrol was in dire short supply in the beachhead with priority going to the Rapier anti-aircraft missile batteries.

ABOVE At 1000 hours on 27 May, 3 PARA started a 24-hour march to Teal Inlet Settlement or in paratrooper parlance a 'tab' or 'Tactical Advance to Battle'. Four hours later 4 Troop began their move to Teal Inlet to accompany 3 PARA following the breakout from Port San Carlos. The weather was atrocious and the terrain appalling, leading to twisted ankles and hypothermia. Such victims were carried on the engine decks of the CVR(T) to dry out and receive hot tea and coffee from the vehicles' BVs.

The move eastwards – 'tabbing' and 'yomping'

As Lieutenant Coreth observed:

We hit a logistical problem that was to dog us throughout the campaign – fuel. We were to support 3 PARA on their long tab to Teal Inlet. It was discovered that there were not enough jerrycans for our fuel. Ordered to stay behind, we went on a hunt. The vehicles rolled at 1400 hours and the Sappers discovered they were missing 28 jerrycans.

BELOW The CVR(T)s of 3 Troop cross the San Carlos River estuary as they escort HQ 3 Commando Brigade and its Bandvagn 202 'Band Wagon' All Terrain Vehicles to Teal Inlet. By 4 June, the bulk of the brigade was in position along the Mount Challenger and Mount Kent ridgeline in preparation for the major battles of 11/12 June.

Using customary cavalry flair, they acquired fuel wherever they could find it – petrol given by islanders or left behind by retreating Argentinians. Having spent ten days in the beachhead to no great effect, 4 Troop crossed the San Carlos River and advanced with 3 PARA to Estancia House without any mobility difficulties where they established an OP on 1 June from where the troop leader declared: 'We could observe Stanley with its famous nightlife, discos, bars and hundreds of pretty girls.'

Meanwhile, 3 Troop remained in the beachhead preparing for their move eastward. 'Suddenly it came over the air that Argy jets were only 10 miles away and closing,' recounted Lieutenant Innes-Ker.

I don't think I have ever run so fast for my vehicle. We just managed to get to a fire position before four jets came in from the west to attack the LSLs. It was a stirring sight. The air was full of missiles and bullets, big and small, of both ours and theirs. I never saw so much firepower being put into a small area in such a short space of time. It was all over in a matter of seconds.

The troop was then ordered to support Paras and Marines 'tabbing' and 'yomping' eastwards on the long march to Port Stanley following the sinking of the SS *Atlantic Conveyor* on 25 May and with it the majority of the Task Force's Chinook helicopters. They also acted as escort to the Royal Marine BV 202 and Snow Trac All-Terrain Vehicles of brigade headquarters on the 30km trek to Teal Inlet. Many of these vehicles got bogged or broke down in the dark but were mostly rescued by 3 Troop with the kinetic towropes of their CVR(T)s. The journey, described by the troop leader as 'resembling the M4 westbound on a Friday evening', took nearly 18 hours. The eventful journey to Teal Inlet and Estancia House finally convinced the high command of the efficacy of CVR(T)'s cross-country mobility. As a case in point, when one tank commander jumped from his CVR(T), he sank up to his knees in

the boggy ground, yet the vehicle itself had not even broken the crust of the sodden peat. The two troops were now tasked to support 5 Brigade at Bluff Cove. Brigade headquarters estimated that it would take up to 48 hours to get there but The Blues and Royals thought otherwise. With the help of local guides, the nine CVR(T)s negotiated a supposedly impassable track south from Estancia House reaching Bluff Cove in just six hours. As Brigadier Anthony 'Tug' Wilson, Commander of 5 Infantry Brigade, declared of their arrival: 'one of those moments one will never forget. It was a remarkable feat . . . they were one of the success stories of the campaign'.

By 7 June, both 3 and 4 Troops were in the area of Fitzroy and Bluff Cove. On the following day, they were on hand to witness the disaster that befell the LSLs *Sir Galahad* and *Sir Tristram*. Lieutenant Innes-Ker recalled the moment that the Argentine aircraft struck:

As they approached, Lance Corporal of Horse Fisher and Trooper Hastings waved cheerfully to two Harriers as they flew low overhead. Their hearts jumped when they saw they were Skyhawks . . . nearly every weapon fired at the second wave. Trooper Fugatt even managed to empty two sub-machine gun magazines at them . . . Trooper

Tucker hit a Skyhawk with his 30mm cannon, as did Trooper Ford back at Fitzroy. This was the day of the tragedy of RFA Sir Galahad and Sir Tristram. Two Three Bravo and the Samson helped carry the wounded to the 2 PARA Regimental Aid Post.

LEFT The Scimitar of Lance Corporal of Horse Stu Mieklejohn with Trooper Pete Fugatt in the driver's seat negotiates a track over the Smoko Mountains during the masterly passage of 3 and 4 Troops from Teal Inlet to join 5 Infantry Brigade at Bluff Cove. Following the advice of local guides, the CVR(T) undertook the trek in just six hours rather than the two days as expected by the high command. Of note, 'smoko' is an Antipodean term for a 'fag break' also used in the Falkland Islands.

LEFT A Scimitar of 3 Troop is dug-in on the shore of Port Pleasant Bay shortly before the bombing of the LSLs *Sir Galahad* and *Sir Tristram* by Argentine A-4 Skyhawks that caused heavy casualties among the Welsh Guards on board. The CVR(T)s were used to ferry the injured to the RAP that fortunately had just been unloaded from LSL *Sir Galahad*.

ABOVE The Samson recovery vehicle came to grief trying to cross the bridge across the Murrell River to the north of the Two Sisters hills. The Samson was considerably overweight due to the amount of ammunition being carried forward for the Scorpions and Scimitars. The vehicle was recovered by Chinook Bravo November and flown to Port Stanley after the end of hostilities.

RIGHT A Sea King flies in with a spare fuel pannier for Callsign Two Four after the previous one split dumping petrol into the vehicle. The Scimitars of the troop are on air defence watch with their Rarden cannons elevated in readiness while supporting the Scots Guards near Fitzroy Settlement. Note the nearest Scimitar still has the wading hose to the oil cooler louvres.

The Welsh Guards suffered 97 casualties in a matter of seconds. The battalion was rendered ineffective until it was reinforced by two companies of 40 Commando RM flown in from San Carlos.

Nevertheless, the calamity did not delay the final offensive against the line of hills overlooking Port Stanley that was scheduled for 11 June. It had taken almost two weeks to concentrate the assault troops, artillery, supplies and vast quantities of ammunition in the area of Mount Kent. The daily supplies for each brigade weighed 150,000kg and a further 46,000kg of ammunition. The Scorpions and Scimitars were redeployed northwards with 3 Troop to support 2 PARA in their assault on Wireless Ridge and 4 Troop with 2 Scots Guard against Mount Tumbledown. Both attacks were scheduled for the night of 13/14 June, both objectives were adjacent to each other and the final barrier

before Port Stanley. Lieutenant Innes-Ker described the journey:

We set off for 2 PARA's position and after about 4 miles we got to Murrell Bridge. I had been warned that we may be too heavy for it so I got out and tested it. I didn't like it at all and wasn't going to cross it, but Lance Corporal Mitchell assured me he could do it so off we went and by God, the bridge bent. It was being pushed to its limits and there was no way Two Eight [Samson] would be able to cross it, with its extra weight being about 2 tons heavier than us.

The inevitable happened and the bridge collapsed under the Samson. As the only recovery vehicle on the islands, this presented an interesting dilemma but the ARV was subsequently retrieved from the river by the Chinook helicopter Bravo November and flown underslung to Port Stanley after the ceasefire.

The battle of the hills

Meanwhile, 3 Troop had joined up with 2 PARA near Estancia House where preparations were being made for the assault on Wireless Ridge. This time 2 PARA demanded a comprehensive fire support plan beyond what they had received at Goose Green. To this end, Major Chris Keeble, the 2i/c of 2 PARA, co-opted Captain Robert

Field of The Blues and Royals to advise on the deployment of 3 Troop in the forthcoming attack. To this end, 3 Troop reconnoitred fire positions within 300m of the Argentinian lines while the CVR(T) passive night sights were highly effective at locating enemy positions for future attention by 2 PARA. During this activity, Callsign Two Three Alpha struck a crater and the vehicle commander, Lance Corporal of Horse Dunkley, was knocked unconscious with much loss of blood. His place was taken by Captain Field who recalled:

I asked the gunner, Trooper Ford, for a quick revision of 30mm [Rarden] misfire drills. He pointed out that it was I who had taught him gunnery in the first place! If Callsign Two Three Bravo's gunnery was not good, I had only myself to blame. It was a bright moonlit night, with a deep frost as we moved back to the battle – quite eerie with the distant chatter of machine guns and bursting illuminations. The only movement was that of small groups of stretcher-bearers, dark against the white carpet, carrying their sad loads. Exhausted, they put down their stretchers to exchange a brief word of greeting as we passed. It was as one imagined a First World War battlefield, not one of the 1980s. The constant whine of artillery shells, the harsh backdrop, small groups of men huddled together for shelter and warmth, others moving gently forward for the next attack. . . . We moved from the ridge line to join in the shoot onto the main part of Wireless Ridge. The Troop was doing a good job. Callsign Two Three Alpha devised a new form of engagement. A short burst of machine-gun fire. The Argentinians usually fired back. The cars would hit the source of the enemy tracer; that particular position would not fire again. Anything that moved or fired at us was 'zapped' and the real star was the Rarden 30mm gun. The Rarden, with its flat trajectory, its six-shot capability and incredible accuracy could neutralise a target very quickly. The HE and APSE (Armour-Piercing Secondary Effects) rounds were used to good effect. . . . We stood off at about 800m from the enemy

and with our GPMGs were able to put sustained bursts of fire into their positions. Trooper Round, my driver, while not on his stomach trying to replace the accelerator pedal which had decided that this was an excellent moment to fall off, played a crucial part in target acquisition. The prize though must go in this respect to the incredible night sight. Fire orders changed, even before 2 PARA's attack, from 'Maggie (coaxial machine gun) traverse left' to 'Running Argentinians'. Tracer floated over our heads from, as it turned out, .50 MGs firing armour-piercing rounds. We also came under intermittent fire from 20mm anti-aircraft guns. None of the vehicles were hit. D Company, 2 PARA, successfully attacked the Ridge and suffered few casualties, a fact possibly due to the support of The Blues and Royals.

In a series of coordinated attacks, the final range of hills overlooking Port Stanley were captured during the nights of 11–14 June. Mount William fell to 1/7th Gurkha Rifles; 3 PARA took Mount Longdon; 45 Commando Two Sisters; 42 Commando Mount Harriet;

BELOW A Scorpion of 3 Troop passes the impact point of an Argentine 155mm shell in the Bluff Cove quarry area showing how the peaty soil absorbed much of the explosive effect and the low water table beneath the surface. Such terrain proved no impediment to CVR(T).

RIGHT The Scorpion Callsign Two Four lies broken and bent on the morning after the mine strike of 14 June at the foot of Mount Tumbledown. Note that the track has turned back on itself due to the height that the vehicle was lifted by the blast that fortunately was somewhat diminished by the soft peaty ground. The vehicle was declared unserviceable once it was found that the BV was inoperable.

Welsh Guards Sapper Hill; and the climactic battles for Wireless Ridge by 2 PARA and Mount Tumbledown by 2nd Scots Guards. The latter assault was preceded by a diversionary attack by G Company from the obvious southerly approach along the line of the Bluff Cove to Port Stanley track. This operation was supported by 4 Troop as recounted by Lieutenant Mark Coreth:

We moved forward to give fire support. About 1km short of my intended position there was a huge crater in the road. Since we were under artillery fire I knew this could be a shell hole, so I decided to risk the possibility of mines. There followed the most incredible explosion – we had hit a mine. The wagon flew into the air and Lance Corporal Farmer failed his flying test for he crashed on landing. Shaken but not stirred, we all had roaring headaches for the next few days. The smell of smoke and burning cordite helped speed up our evacuation of the vehicle. The wagon was a shambles. The driver's hatch was blown off, as were the sprockets and some road wheels, the hull was buckled and the turret a mess. With shells falling and little point in hanging about, I sent Lance Corporals Lambert and Farmer back to the Regimental Aid Post. The other vehicles pulled forward and we began to fire as best we could onto the enemy positions.

This involved the invention of new techniques, untaught at Gunnery School.

BELOW The Chinook HC1 'Bravo November' (ZA718 of 18 Squadron) lifts the mine-damaged Callsign Two Four from Mount Tumbledown to Port Stanley racecourse on 18 June. Bravo November was the sole surviving Chinook after the loss of the SS *Atlantic Conveyor* and flew 109 hours of sorties during the campaign.

Lance Corporals of Horse Ward and Meiklejohn used the previously unheard of '30mm High Explosive at 4,000m technique' and Corporal of Horse Stretton the '76mm Indirect Night Shoot'. I corrected fall of shot from the outside of the vehicles and awarded 'A' grades to all. The battered patrol reappeared, most of them wounded, and were flown back. We settled down for the remainder of the night. An engineer came forward next morning. In a 25m radius around the crater he cleared 57 anti-tank mines. Having discovered that the Welsh Guards were now advancing I took over Two Four Bravo and, leaving Alpha and Charlie to help the Scots Guards pick up their dead, set off in pursuit. The columns of men marching hell-for-leather up that road were an amazing sight. We found the colonel who said that he believed the white flag was flying but wanted me to recce forward to confirm it. We pushed on past endless articles of abandoned equipment, artillery pieces and dead. Finally, we arrived on top of Sapper Hill, the key to Stanley. The war really was over. We were elated. Elation turned to dismay when we were ordered back to the mud hole that was Fitzroy. I and Lance Corporal of Horse Meiklejohn stayed with my vehicle while the others went back to make a camp. While we waited, the minefield was marked with the help of the Argentinians who had laid it.

On the morning of 14 June, 3 Troop was in the vanguard of the British troops after the successful night battles. Captain Field continued:

Daybreak, after a brief ammo replenishment, saw us moving on Stanley, from ridge line to ridge line. Morale was sky-high after the previous night, and there was much discussion about Panhards and what was soon to happen to them. Suddenly it was all over. The Argentinians had surrendered. Our initial reaction was one of disappointment. Adrenalin was flowing, we were looking forward to a really good punch-up. This was followed moments later by an immense surge of

ABOVE With the regimental flag flying, Callsign Two Three Alpha approaches Port Stanley with troops of 2 PARA on 14 July 1982 at the conclusion of the conflict.

BELOW To the victor the spoils – Lieutenant Mark Coreth sits atop an AML 90 with Lance Corporal Kevin Lambert and Lance Corporal Ged Farmer in the driver's seat as the Samson tows the armoured car to a landing craft ready for embarking on HMS *Fearless* for the journey back to the UK. Two captured AML 90s of the *Escuadron de Exploracion Caballeria Blindada* 181 were returned to the UK with one retained by The Blues and Royals and the other at the Tank Museum, Bovington.

103

relief and delight; we had survived. With the MILAN Platoon loaded on to our vehicles, the dash for Stanley began. The vehicles, surrounded and covered by members of 2 PARA, The Blues and Royals' flag proudly flying, we drove into Stanley. We were exuberant. We reached the War Memorial on the outskirts, in the lead by now where we were told to stop. We stopped. I hoisted the Union Jack from the antenna of my vehicle, we waited. One by one the heads disappeared, the hatches closed, the Troop slept, exhausted, drained, woken only by the chill of a late afternoon and a feeling of great anti-climax. 3 Troop moved next day into a comfortable house and captured masses of trophies, including two Panhard armoured vehicles. 4 Troop moved up after a few days from Fitzroy to join 3 Troop and go aboard HMS Fearless.

Above all, the Falklands land campaign was an infantry war as Lieutenant Colonel Hew Pike, CO of 3 PARA, recounted later:

The battles to capture key objectives, all but Goose Green fought at night, were the very essence of the infantry's contribution to victory and the ultimate test of each attacking battalion's courage and fighting power.

The story of each battle is well known. What is perhaps most interesting are the unchanging lessons of such battles, all of which would have been familiar to our fathers and grandfathers. Yet no one, in either brigade, from brigadier downwards, had any experience of such actions, and no amount of history is a substitute for experience. Above all, I believe, the Falklands impressed upon us all just how long such battles can take and hence how important is the sustained rate of all forms of direct and indirect fire to success, in breaking the enemy's will. . . . Even more so it was the junior leader, at platoon-, section-, and fire team-level, who faced his supreme test. Here, example was everything if men were to keep moving and outmanoeuvre enemy trenches or bunkers.

The fight-through often proved a long,

costly process. At very close quarters with the enemy, every resource of field craft and weaponry was needed to take out each position. More often crawling than running or standing, grenades, both HE and phosphorus – the latter much more effective – and the light anti-tank weapon, were used to cause at least momentary shock and some casualties, so that each small assault group could close with the position and kill those remaining. Their movements were closely tied in with supporting fire from MILAN and GPMG (SF) fire teams, whilst mortar and artillery fire was also used with increasing skill and accuracy, very close indeed to our own assaulting groups.

This murderous phase of battle was made worse by the frequent attentions of enemy artillery which tracked the progress of attacking forces with uncanny accuracy. In the mountains, fixed heavy machine gun positions and skilled snipers also represented particularly lethal threats. In one instance, on Mount Longdon, a three-man MILAN crew was killed by one 105mm recoilless rifle round, as they tried to move to a better supporting position. The capture of Goose Green, Mount Longdon, Two Sisters, Mount Harriet, Mount Tumbledown and Wireless Ridge, proved the will of the attackers over that of the defenders.

These bloody encounters with the enemy, physically and mentally draining, demonstrated that the training and courage of the British Infantry of the 1980s was equal at least to that of earlier generations. . . . One particularly significant feature of the campaign was the performance of the CVR(T)s of The Blues and Royals. Commanders were cautious about ordering them forward over such unpredictable terrain, but their troop leaders and crews had no such doubts. Determined to prove their value, they negotiated the rolling, windswept hills and valleys with great skill, and although night movement proved generally inadvisable, by day they rapidly closed with their infantry comrades, eager to support them in whatever tasks lay ahead.

ABOVE Callsign Two Four 02FD76 lies forlornly on Port Stanley racecourse before its return to UK where it was rebuilt as a Sabre.

LEFT Lieutenant Mark Coreth stands in the turret of 02FD96 during the Falklands victory parade of The Blues and Royals through their hometown of Windsor.

Chapter Five

CVR(T) in combat – Operation Granby, 1991

During the Gulf War of 1991, the Iraqi Army failed entirely in the basic tenets of manoeuvre warfare. Tanks were invariably dug into prepared positions that denied them the fundamental asset of mobility. They proved highly vulnerable to air attack but it was the devastating volume of artillery fire that proved their nemesis during the land campaign.

OPPOSITE A Spartan of Support Troop, A Squadron QDG, with a mini pipe fascine strapped to its side, approaches an abandoned Iraqi modified T-55, which is about to be destroyed by the Assault Pioneers of 12 Field Support Squadron RE on board the Spartan.

Operation Granby

On 2 August 1990, Iraqi armed forces invaded the sovereign state of Kuwait. Spearheaded by two armoured divisions of the Republican Guard, the country was occupied within 24 hours. The Iraqi dictator, Saddam Hussein, declared Kuwait to be henceforth the 19th province of Iraq. International condemnation was swift and an armed response was authorised by the United Nations at the behest of the United States, supported by fellow Security Council members Britain and France. Despite months of negotiations, Saddam Hussein remained intransigent declaring: 'The Iraqi people are capable of fighting to the victorious end which Allah decrees . . . the blood of our martyrs will burn you!'

Just four days after the invasion, elements of the 82nd US Airborne Division landed in Saudi Arabia, including 51 Sheridan Armored Reconnaissance/Airborne Assault Vehicles (AR/AAV), as part of Operation Desert Shield. On 14 September, the British government announced Operation Granby with the deployment of 7 Armoured Brigade Group, the Desert Rats, under the command of Brigadier Patrick Cordingley. It comprised two armoured regiments equipped with Challenger MBTs and a mechanised infantry regiment with Warrior IFVs. The units entailed were the Royal Scots Dragoon Guards, the Queen's Royal Irish Hussars and 1st Battalion The Staffordshire Regiment. Since an armoured brigade had no integral medium reconnaissance component, A Squadron of 1st The Queen's Dragoon Guards (QDG) was attached to fulfil that function. On 10 October, advance parties of the Brigade Group departed for the Gulf and by the end of the month 80% of its personnel and much equipment had arrived in theatre.

With unstinting support from the regiment as a whole, A Squadron QDG underwent frenzied preparations before its CVR(T) vehicles were loaded aboard the SS *Mercandian Queen II* at Bremerhaven on 27 September. As a STUFT (Ship Taken Up from Trade), the vessel was a veritable rust bucket that broke down repeatedly en route. She finally docked at Al Jubayl on the evening of 26 October and the squadron deployed to the desert three days later. The Desert Rats were initially attached to the 1st US Marine Division to augment its armour strength. With admirable generosity, the Marines provided considerable logistical support to 7th Armoured Brigade Group before the British Force Maintenance Area (FMA) was fully established.

As the commander of A Squadron QDG, Major Hamish Macdonald formed a close rapport with the Marines that proved highly

**RIGHT 'ROSCREA',
a Scorpion of the
Reconnaissance Troop
of the Queen's Royal
Irish Hussars (QRIH),
stands at the dockside
at Al Jubayl as the
units of 7 Armoured
Brigade arrive in Kuwait
in October 1990. All
the AFVs of QRIH were
named after towns and
villages in Ireland.**

propitious, culminating in a hard-fought rugby match. Thereafter, the Marines adopted 'The Welsh Cavalry' as part of their own. Early troop training was undertaken at Al Fadili, some 50km west of Al Jubayl. Suffice to say that the squadron's CVR(T)s were of a similar age to most of their crews but, despite some apprehension, the vehicles performed well in the new-found desert conditions. Similarly, the personnel quickly adapted to the daunting expanse of the terrain and the speed of movement that was possible as compared to the close topography of north-west Europe.

In the second week of November, the brigade undertook Exercise Jubayl Rat when a number of manoeuvres were practised, including the rupture of a 5km-deep obstacle zone and then a breakout, involving the firing of both direct and indirect weapons. The exercise ended on 16 November when the Brigade Group was declared operational for battle. It highlighted the problem of medium reconnaissance operating within range of battle group sensors and weapon systems. The need to give recce space to operate was clearly realised but it is questionable whether this lesson was actually taken fully to heart. Six days later, the decision was taken to deploy 4 Armoured Brigade, comprising the 14th/20th King's Hussars (14/20H) equipped with Challenger MBT and two armoured infantry battalions, 1st Battalion, The Royal Scots (1RS) and 3rd Battalion, The Royal Regiment of Fusiliers (3RFF) that were both equipped with Warrior IFV. Since this was an infantry-heavy formation, it should more correctly be designated a mechanised brigade and indeed the MoD referred to it throughout the campaign as 4 Brigade. However, both had served together in North Africa during the Second World War and both adopted the jerboa as their brigade insignia to be known to all and sundry as The Desert Rats. The 4 Armoured Brigade were joined by other major units and deployed to the Gulf to form 1st (British) Armoured Division, under the command of Major General Rupert Smith. It was to be established in theatre during early January 1991 and be operational by the end of the month: a daunting prospect by any standards.

Among the reinforcements under Operation Granby 1.5 was a reconnaissance regiment,

the 16th/5th, The Queen's Royal Lancers (QRL), to provide medium reconnaissance for the division. Based at Herford in Germany, the regiment was tasked on 22 November for deployment to the Gulf and within two weeks its CVR(T) vehicles were on the high seas. Its personnel started to arrive from 16 December onwards and were based at Blackadder Camp at Al Jubayl to await their CVR(T)s. The latter began unloading at the docks in Al Jubayl on New Year's Day and desert training began immediately with the UN deadline of 15 January for Iraqi withdrawal from Kuwait looming. At the same time, A Squadron QDG was attached to the 16th/5th QRL in order to consolidate all reconnaissance assets and also to pass on the experience of two months in the desert.

The QRL comprised an RHQ and three Sabre Squadrons (A, B, C and HQ) while A Squadron QDG constituted a fourth reinforced Sabre Squadron. Major Alick Finlayson, 2i/c 16th/5th Lancers, recalls:

The original idea was to have an RHQ and a squadron for each of the brigades and the remaining two squadrons as divisional medium reconnaissance. We had not practised recce in attack [in BAOR] and all our training had been for recce by stealth. However General Smith had developed the concept of having two manoeuvre brigades [7th and 4th] and a depth strike brigade based on the artillery and a recce strike force. Recce was to set out ahead of the manoeuvre brigades and locate the enemy's depth and reserve formations, which would then be kept at arm's length by being attacked by artillery and air while the manoeuvre brigades got on with the contact battle.

In the words of General Rupert Smith their role was: 'To attack the enemy in such a way as to prevent him firing and moving to reinforce the Contact Battle, aiming to delay, disrupt and destroy him.'

Accordingly, the QRL was placed under control of the Divisional Artillery Group commanded by Brigadier Ian Drurie as CRA (Commander Royal Artillery). He split his

LEFT AND ABOVE All the battle groups were assigned air defence batteries of Spartans equipped with Javelin SAM operators. Due to complete coalition air supremacy, the Javelin was not used in action. The shoulder-launched SAM is visible on the ground to the right of these three Spartans of 12 Air Defence Regiment RA, flying prominent Union flags as their own form of air defence.

assets into three functions – the Air Defence Group, the Direct (or Close) Support Group and the Depth Fire Group, responsible for the prosecution of the Depth Battle, with the QRL being part of the latter. The principal weapons for the Depth Fire Group were the M-270 Multiple Launch Rocket System (MLRS) Phase 1 of 39 Heavy (39 Hy) Regiment RA and the M-110 8in (203mm) Self-Propelled Howitzers of 32 Heavy (32 Hy) Regiment RA. It was also intended that the M-109 155mm Self-Propelled Howitzers of 26 Field Regiment RA would take part in the Depth Battle but in the event they were tasked to supporting the Contact Battle.

The limitations of CVR(T) were well known and well founded in the Gulf with the soft sand of Kuwait causing electrical problems, such as ingress into contact breakers and air

LEFT 'THE UNTOUCHABLES', a Spartan of 10 (Assaye) Battery, takes part in an exercise at Concentration Area Keyes in early February 1991. The Prussian Eagle on the side above the vehicle name indicates that this Air Defence Spartan is acting in support of the 14th/20th King's Hussars within 4 Armoured Brigade. A total of 72 Air Defence Spartans were deployed to the Gulf with a proportion held in War Maintenance Reserve.

filters, while the hard-packed gravel terrain of Iraq imposed its own mobility difficulties. Above all, CVR(T)s lacked adequate Night Observation Devices (NOD) that were suitable for the desert environment, compounded by the basic problem of navigation in such open and desolate terrain. The latter was addressed by the introduction of the Global Positioning System (GPS) that was to be fundamental to the success of the whole campaign. Several devices were issued, such as Magellan or Trimpack, and these transformed desert operations particularly at night. As state-of-the-art technology, there were never sufficient numbers to satisfy all requirements.

GPS came as a revelation to Captain Richard Wootton commanding the Reconnaissance Platoon of the Staffords Battle Group:

Trimpack was undoubtedly a battle-winner for us. It meant that we could move accurately by day and night, in all weather conditions. The battle group could carry out complex manoeuvres and you could be sure that everyone would end up in exactly the right position. We were issued with two in the platoon, which limited us to an extent, but at least I could split the platoon into two halves if I needed to. All you had to do was press a button and it would give you ten-figure grid reference of your exact location. You could also programme in the grid of a position you wanted to move to, and it would tell you which way to go; you know, left a bit, right a bit, and so on. It would tell you how far you had to run as you were going; it was an excellent bit of kit. At certain times, usually twice a day, it would go down when the satellites were out of alignment. But that would only last for half an hour or so.

Similarly, the Clansman radio equipment of CVR(T) was upgraded with the installation of BID300 that allowed communications instantly in clear secure speech that was a vast improvement over the previous BATCO system. Of equal importance was the acquisition of NODs and battlefield surveillance equipment. These included OTIS and MSTAR (Manportable Surveillance and Target Acquisition Radar). Unfortunately, neither could be mounted on a vehicle while in motion so were largely redundant in a fast-moving battle. The NOD of choice was Spyglass – a hand-held thermal imager with a day/night capability and an acquisition range of 2.5km. Thus, the

RIGHT Just prior to the land campaign, 1st (British) Armoured Division conducted two major exercises to practise the initial advance over the border into Iraq. The first, called Exercise Dibdibah Drive, rehearsed the 'passage of lines' of moving some 1,500 vehicles of the division through the breach in the Iraqi lines. Here, the AFVs of the 16th/5th The Queen's Royal Lancers stretch into the distance as they await their orders to move.

major enhancements of CVR(T) in the Gulf were GPS, BID and TI NOD, although Alvis did propose an up-armouring kit for CVR(T) but at 1 ton it would have overburdened the already heavily laden vehicle.

With the failure of Saddam Hussein to comply with the UN deadline for withdrawal, the air bombardment of Iraq began at midnight GMT on 16 January. Ten days later, 1st (BR) Armoured Division was attached to VII (US) Corps, which consisted of 1st Infantry Division (Mechanized), 1st Cavalry Division (Armored), the 1st and 3rd Armored Divisions, 1st (BR) Armoured Division, 2nd Armored Cavalry Regiment and the 11th Aviation Brigade. The British acted as the right flank protection for the Corps with 1st and 3rd Armored Divisions as the main strike force. 1st (BR) Armoured Division and VII (US) Corps combined to support the main offensive against the Republican Guard. This entailed moving the complete division and its logistic train 217 miles (350km) westwards to Concentration Area Keyes, some 50 miles (80km) south of the point at which the borders of Kuwait, Iraq and Saudi Arabia meet. There the division was declared fully operational on 1 February. At this stage, the Recce Group acted as a screen to the north of Keyes in case of any Iraqi incursion similar to that at the Saudi Arabian town of Khafji that occurred at the end of January.

The division undertook its final preparations with two major field training exercises, Dibdibah Drive and Dibdibah Charge, to rehearse the breach crossing and passage of lines. In the meantime, A Squadron QDG participated in a series of artillery raids along the Iraqi border. These were conducted along the complete coalition front in close conjunction with the air campaign. They were intended to destroy high-value Iraqi targets, assess enemy reaction and encourage deserters for intelligence purposes. The first artillery raid took place on 18 February involving 32 Hy and 39 Hy Regiments with A Squadron QDG providing route marking and securing of the artillery firing sites. The CVR(T)s also guided and protected the guns as they withdrew after the fire mission. The concept relied upon the ability of the artillery Fireplan Group to deploy rapidly into forward gun positions that had been plotted by the CVR(T)s, conduct a short fire mission and then withdraw before any enemy counterbattery reaction with CVR(T)s acting as the rearguard. These raids continued until 23 February when the squadron was regrouped with 16/5th QRL in the staging area. The weeks and months of training and preparations were finally over.

Operation Desert Sabre

G Day – at 1000 hours on the morning of 24 February, Major General Rupert Smith held an Orders Group for the commanders of 1st (BR) Armoured Division. Based on the available intelligence, the GOC had identified a series of objectives, each of which was

THE ATTACK ON OBJECTIVE COPPER SOUTH

At dawn on 26 February 1991, the Fusiliers Battle Group attacked Objective Copper South in conjunction with the 14th/20th King's Hussars. The demoralised enemy was quick to give up but one position had to be cleared by dismounted troops of the Recce Group. Despite surrendering, one Iraqi soldier suddenly returned fire with his AK-47. With great presence of mind, Fusilier Cassar as the driver of MCT(S) Four One Bravo grabbed his SA80. Tony Cassar recalled: 'We approached the position because an Iraqi was trying to surrender. While my vehicle commander [Dave Weaver] got out with the Jock [Derrick McManus] to see to him I had a look about and

realised that we were on the edge of what looked like a platoon-sized position. Fearing RPGs I told the MILAN operator Pete Nelson to scan with his MILAN post. I reached back for my rifle losing my helmet in the process. I then went to scanning the position. Dave and the Jock were behind me. I heard firing and turned round to see the two guys under fire. I saw where the fire was coming from and took aim and fired twice. The enemy soldier fell from view. I remember thinking at the time that I had always disliked the Fig 12 target because it was so small and my first ever shot in anger was at a Fig 12. All this while pulling the trigger.' *(RRF and David Rowlands)*

named after a particular metal. These were to be attacked sequentially by the armoured brigades with the divisional artillery supporting each respective assault. Accordingly, pressure was to be maintained on the enemy in a constant unremitting offensive of fire and movement. Meanwhile, the Recce Group was to conduct the Depth Battle to isolate and degrade Iraqi reserves through attrition by artillery and air bombardment.

Following the breaching of the Iraqi defences by 1st (US) Mechanized Infantry Division, 7 Armoured Brigade broke out of the bridgehead at 1515 hours on G+1 followed shortly by 4 Armoured Brigade. Contrary to the initial plan, the Recce Group was not released first, so the QRL did not cross the New Jersey Start Line until 1500 hours. As Major Alick Finlayson recalled: 'The 16/5th moved out of the breach at the same time as 7th Brigade but had to go in a wide loop to the west and north on to the first objective, Copper, whereas 7th Brigade could go straight there.' Both arrived at Copper at much the same time, thus the Recce Group were denied their first depth target. The commander of B Squadron QRL, Major Richard Quicke, observed:

The role of the depth fire brigade was that, while the active manoeuvre brigade was attacking an objective, recce would loop round to the next objective, or find the

enemy's reserves in depth, and bring down artillery and air, thus 'Kicking the enemy in the balls while hitting him on the nose'. This concept fell apart from the outset. 16/5th arrived at the staging area on the night of G Day-1. They expected an imminent move forward, but the US were worried about fratricide, so UK 1 Div were held until noon of G+1. We were launched from the breach towards Copper, but were then retasked to hit [Objective] Zinc. At around 1900 we stopped in squadron hides north-west of Zinc.

So far, the QRL had not fired a shot in anger.

In the meantime, 7 Armoured Brigade had launched its attack against Objective Copper that lay some 30km from the New Jersey Start Line. The first hour of the advance was uneventful as the commander of the Staffords Reconnaissance Platoon, Captain Richard Wootton, recalled:

We'd been moving at a cracking pace and I was thinking, well there's absolutely nothing here. Then the lead squadron reported some enemy on our northern boundary. The CO [Lieutenant Colonel Charles Rogers] tasked me to go, and I gave orders over the net for half the platoon to deal with it, and we set off. Half the Mobile MILAN followed us as well, and I thought this was pretty good teamwork. They did it without being told and off we went. In fact the CO gave me a bollocking on the air; he said, 'You're not moving yet, why not?' I said we were 'fire and manoeuvring', because we were moving off into territory that we didn't know. That is, keeping one vehicle static and observing, covering the other one as it moves forward, and then when it stops, leapfrogging the other past it and so on. But we just couldn't move quickly enough like that, so we all had to move at the same time. That went against the grain.

Then we had a report that there might be a vehicle there as well, so it was a little more worrying. I kept looking at the satnav as we moved, and we were starting to go outside the boundary into the American area, and all of a sudden you think: I hope the Americans aren't coming up on my flank. Anyway, it turned out to be three Iraqis who claimed to have been captured by the Americans already. Of course we went through all the proper drills for taking prisoners, because we'd heard that some of them had got Claymore mines attached to them and were suicide bombers. As we were dealing with them, what should

come from our west but three Apache helicopters and that was quite frightening. They do look like big wasps and they're quite aggressive. They were about 2km away and I was pretty sure that they would see our IFF, Identification Friend or Foe, markers. Those were inverted Vs painted on the vehicle and a big luminous panel on the back of the turret.

Dealing with the prisoners was a time-consuming business, and the Battle Group wanted to press on. We got a message to just leave them there, so we gave them a bit of food. I gave one of them a cigarette because he asked for one. In fact, I was feeling compassionate towards them so I gave them a packet, which I came to regret a couple of days later! They were in a miserable state; they wanted to be taken, but we had to leave them there.

In the event there was no resistance on Objective Copper. It was a portent of things to come. No 7 Armoured Brigade was now tasked to assault Objective Zinc where the 16/5th QRL were awaiting their orders to bombard the position.

BELOW The vehicles of A Squadron QDG circle the wagons as Squadron Headquarters is set up during the course of the land campaign. A total of 503 CVR(T) variants were deployed to the Gulf including 238 Spartan, 101 Scimitar, 33 Scorpion, 32 Samson, 24 Sultan, 22 Striker, 23 MCT Spartan and 20 Samaritan, as well as four Stormer VLMSS. An availability rate of 80% was achieved throughout the campaign because the resources, particularly spares, were to hand.

The divisional concept for the use of medium reconnaissance was that of Recce Strike whereby elements of the 16th/5th The Queen's Royal Lancers were to advance swiftly in order to attack enemy depth or reserve formations with indirect fire while the brigades engaged in the Contact Battle. The only occasion that this concept met with complete success was with A Squadron, 1st The Queen's Dragoon Guards, in the attack on Objective Lead – an Iraqi regimental-sized position of mainly dug-in tanks and certain manoeuvre units that could conceivably interfere with the Contact Battle. As dawn broke on 26 February 1991, A Squadron began to bombard Objective Lead with the full panoply of artillery and close-support aircraft, including A-10 Warthogs shown here flying in from the left to engage the dug-in tanks in the distance. The Spartan PFAC or Principal Forward Air Controller at extreme left guides them using Target Laser Markers obtained from the USMC. Below the A-10 is the Squadron Headquarters of A Squadron, QDG, with the squadron commander, Major Hamish Macdonald, in the Sultan command vehicle with the rear door open. Behind it is the Ferret Mark1/2 of the Squadron LO, Lieutenant Mark Matthews, while the other Sultan, Zero Delta, acts as the alternative Command Vehicle. In the far background Multiple Rocket Launched System (MLRS) obliterates Iraqi opposition, acre by acre. To the right, the Strikers of the Guided Weapon Troop engage other targets with Swingfire ATGW with some notable long-range kills.

(QDG and David Rowlands)

Advance to contact

Meanwhile, 4th Armoured Brigade began its advance at 1930 hours in asymmetrical formation with the 14th/20th King's Hussars Battle Group leading, followed by that of the 1st Battalion, The Royal Scots and the 3rd Battalion, The Royal Regiment of Fusiliers, bringing up the rear in reserve. At the head of the Fusiliers Battle Group was the Reconnaissance Platoon in their CVR(T) whose image intensification sights were inadequate in the prevailing conditions. Its commander, Captain Paul Nanson, had to rely on GPS but, not far into the advance, the system ceased to function. He recalls: 'It is difficult to describe the feeling of desolation when the system showed – GPS BAD. You either had to sit and wait for the satellites to return or press on with a Silva compass and hope for the best.' Calling TAC HQ, he reported: 'We've lost the satellites', to which the CO, Lieutenant Colonel Andrew Larpent, responded: 'Keep going, you're doing a great job.' Progress was further compromised by the foul weather with driving rain reducing visibility to virtually nil. Captain Nanson in Callsign Two One led the column, Sergeant Ian Oliver in Two Two, some 5m to his left and Corporal Dave Stanier in Two One Alpha to his right. Sergeant 'Ollie' Oliver recalls:

The weather was so bad that even with NVGs [night vision goggles] I could hardly see the end of the Rarden cannon, so I was all the more surprised when Corporal Stanier reported on the radio that he could see some vehicles at a distance of 1km and found that he was using his OTIS sight fixed to the turret roof, which was only supposed to be mounted when the vehicle was stationary. However, any form of vision was vital to maintain the advance but even thermal imaging was seriously degraded in such conditions.

The Raven image intensification sights of the Warriors were rendered almost useless because of the total lack of starlight and their commanders had to travel with their heads out of their turrets to be able to see anything. They were soon sodden and chilled to the bone, despite their body armour and NBC suits. Periodically they had to wipe the gunners' optics to allow them some vision. As for the drivers, their periscopes were soon totally obscured with caked sand that the wipers were unable to dislodge. To steer they had to be directed by their commanders, whose only sense of direction was provided by the dim glow of red lights on the back of the vehicle in front. Corporal John Mulheran of 7 Platoon 3RRF recalled the first night of the advance:

Wet, cold, raining, windy, lots of bangs and flashes, explosions and with everyone on tenterhooks but really confident as they knew what they had to do. It just a matter of when you had to do it. Sometimes we opened the door or top hatches to show the lads the burning tanks or points of interest. All the same, we knew after the first night that we had them on the run.

In the rifle companies, the only vehicles with thermal imaging were those of the Warrior MILAN section that travelled on the flanks of the Recce Group to protect it against armour attack. On the left flank of C Company, Sergeant 'Chinney' Needham spent the whole night with his eye glued to the MIRA sight of the MILAN firing post on the pintle mount above the turret of Callsign Four Three. Soaked to the skin from the lashing rain, his vigilance was vital to the safety of the battle group, as was that of the MILAN gunners of his two companion vehicles, with each carrying a firing post above the turret and one mounted on the open roof hatches. Accordingly, the crew in the rear compartment was open to the elements and soon were equally wet. Every two hours the lithium batteries and cooling gas bottles of the MIRA had to be changed to keep the system working. Meanwhile, in the packed troop compartments of the Warrior section vehicles, most Fusiliers dozed in their 'fart-filled fug' oblivious to the drama unfolding outside.

On the northern axis of the divisional advance, 7 Armoured Brigade was attacking Copper North, which was secured by midnight after a two-hour battle. To the south, the Life Guards Squadron of 14th/20th King's

Hussars and 1st Royal Scots cleared Objective Bronze without casualties: a fact that was greeted with relief as it indicated that the Iraqis were probably unwilling to fight with much determination. Throughout the night, the King's Hussars Battle Group fought against entrenched tank companies on Objective Copper South in an action they later called the Battle of Al Haniyah. It was in this scene of devastation that the Fusiliers Battle Group found itself at daybreak on G+2, which Major Keith Kiddie, as 2i/c of 3RRF, recounted:

As the light came up, it was like being on the set of a Hollywood movie, all the war films you've ever seen rolled into one. Depth fire was in progress and there were tanks on their sides on fire, hulks of things burning and exploding in a very theatrical way.

It was the first occasion that many Fusiliers were able to dismount since the start of the offensive and even in the midst of such destruction there were sights to gladden the eye. Major Kiddie was somewhat circumspect when he heard his driver, Fusilier Dave Greenhaugh, say 'Boss, come here and look at this.' Not known as 'Lord Wellhard' for nothing, Major Kiddie expected his driver to have found some hideously mutilated Iraqi but in fact he was shown an exquisite flower that had blossomed in the desert after the night of rain.

As the battle group paused on Copper South, the Reconnaissance Group moved forward to screen the formation and set up the forming-up point (FUP) for the forthcoming attack on Objective Brass. During the move eastwards, half of the Reconnaissance Platoon, comprising four Scimitars and two MCTS Spartans under the command of Colour Sergeant Mick McCarthy, was screening the left flank when it encountered the battle group's first moving Iraqi AFV as an MTLB tried to escape across their front. Corporal Pete Cockerill in Callsign Two Three reacted with alacrity and cried 'Sabot on!'; Colour Sergeant McCarthy shouted 'Fire!' and three rounds struck the MTLB. It shuddered to a halt. At the same moment, a MILAN missile from Four One Alpha screamed past Two Three and hit the MTLB, causing it to burst into flames. Over the net was heard: 'Two Three, this is Four

One Alpha. Thanks for the spotting rounds. Target's destroyed.'

Soon thereafter, the first Iraqi infantry began to surrender to the Reconnaissance Platoon. However, not all the Iraqis were willing to capitulate without a fight. Corporal Derrick McManus of The Queen's Own Highlanders in the CVR(T) Scimitar Callsign Two Three Alpha encountered an English-speaking Iraqi close to a command bunker. Ordering him to tell those inside to surrender, McManus lost patience when he returned after ten minutes and shrugged. Under the covering L37 machine gun of Corporal Dave 'Gatling' Weaver in MCTS Spartan Callsign Four One Bravo, McManus threw an L2A2 grenade into the bunker doorway while taking cover behind his Scimitar. After the explosion, both McManus and Weaver moved forward of the vehicle to see the result. As they did, the sand around their feet began to spurt. At first, McManus thought that Weaver had had a negligent discharge when the 30mm Rarden cannon cracked just inches from his head, until he realised that they were in fact under fire. Despite wearing his helmet and noise-attenuating headphones, McManus was to suffer partial deafness and a severe headache for the rest of the war. The gunner, Lance Corporal Russell, had engaged a trench from where an Iraqi had opened fire with a Kalashnikov but the sabot round ricocheted away. Corporal McManus then tried to eliminate him with a CLAW grenade, but the fire from the trench continued and both he and Weaver rushed back to their vehicles.

In MCTS Spartan Callsign Four One Delta, Corporal Geoff Green witnessed the scene: 'It was like the Keystone Cops. There were the two NCOs running around their vehicles trying to get back in, trying to get on the radio and let everyone know what was happening but they were panting so much it was impossible to hear what they were saying.' With considerable presence of mind, the driver of Callsign Four One Bravo, Fusilier Anthony Cassar, stood up in his hatch and returned fire with his rifle, shooting the Iraqi soldier dead. As McManus threw himself into the turret of Two Three Alpha head first, he ordered his driver, Lance Corporal Douggie Young, to reverse away from the trench line for fear of RPG anti-armour weapons. Unfortunately, without direction from the commander (who was still trying to right himself in the narrow confines of the turret), Young reversed the Scimitar into the side of the Spartan, Four One Bravo. Confusion turned to panic, as the radios in the rear of the turret fell on McManus and Turner and both felt wet warmth on their legs. Thinking it was blood, they were relieved to find that it was only the BV that had burst open in the collision, covering them in warm water.

Close by, the Support Group commander, Major Corin Pearce, followed the action over the radio. He was only too aware of his orders to prosecute the advance as quickly as possible. However, there were some soft-skinned echelon vehicles of the 14th/20th King's Hussars nearby, which were highly vulnerable to any entrenched Iraqis. He decided to clear the enemy trench system with ground troops. Calling his MILAN platoon commander, Captain Guy Briselden, he ordered him to deploy his MILAN detachments as infantry, almost all of whom were from the Queen's Own Highlanders Regiment. As his three Warriors approached the position, Captain Briselden conferred with his platoon 2i/c, Colour Sergeant 'Jazz' Barrie in the turret of their Warrior, Callsign Four Four. Unfortunately, they had no radio communications with their companion vehicle Four Four Alpha, nor did they have radios to converse with troops on the ground. Captain Briselden then said: 'I'll go first.' Barrie replied 'No, I'll go first.' They decided to dismount together. After firing a six-round clip of HE and sabot at the trench, they flung open their hatches. In moments, Captain Briselden found himself standing on the rear of the Warrior alone, listening to Barrie swearing volubly and struggling to free himself after his body armour had snagged inside the turret.

Laughing all the while, Briselden jumped down to the ground and opened the rear door. Grabbing a bandoleer of grenades, he divided off the men in the back into pairs with himself and Private Low as one and Lance Corporal Symes of the Devon and Dorsets and Private Pearson as the other. Meanwhile, Sergeant Barrie ran some 75m across open ground to brief the other two vehicle commanders and deploy their troops on the ground. As the other two Warriors put down suppressive fire, Briselden briefed his men and then, with a sense of deep apprehension at the unknown, he and Low left the reassuring armour protection of their Warrior and moved off down the side of the vehicle. As he ran forward, Briselden cursed as he realised that his webbing with his bayonet and ammunition was hanging from the driver's mirror. After some 15m, he and Private 'Titch' Low dropped to the ground and began to advance by fire and movement towards the trench. Grasping a hand grenade, Briselden leapt up and ran forward to hurl it over the trench parapet. With a resounding crack, the grenade exploded, sending up a fountain of matter that arced over Briselden and splattered Low, who declared 'Aye boss, and thanks for that.' The grenade had landed in an Iraqi field latrine, sending up a shower of excrement. With the adrenalin still pumping from their initial charge, both fell about laughing.

By now, Sergeant Barrie had organised the Highlanders from the other Warriors into two fire teams, each of five men, under the command of Sergeant Brian 'Scouse' Lammond and Corporal Alan Wicks. Without radios, it was difficult to coordinate the assault but by taking Briselden's four-man team as the centreline, the other two sections moved forward on each side and began to clear the trench system. Meanwhile, 'Titch' Low's rifle had jammed; Captain Briselden proffered his own as he also had a pistol, but Low was soon able to clear his weapon and their team continued the assault. Having purchased a Beretta Model 92FS in Germany before deployment to the Gulf, Captain Briselden decided to use the pistol to clear the next bunker they encountered as it was easier to handle in the confined space. He also wished to conserve his rifle ammunition since the extent of the position remained unknown. By posting a grenade through the embrasure followed by several rounds of pistol fire, Briselden cleared several bunkers as he and the Highlanders moved through the extensive trench system. As they advanced, the supporting fire of the two Warriors was becoming uncomfortably close, particularly from Four Alpha. Realising the danger, Sergeant Lammond valiantly ran back to his vehicle, opened the rear door and used the intercom to adjust his gunner's fire on to targets in depth as the assault reached its climax.

In this first encounter with the entrenched enemy – who had had many months to position – the men of the Reconnaissance Group showed considerable fortitude and commendable spirit. Many Iraqis subsequently surrendered. For his inspirational leadership in this exploit of arms that delayed the advance only momentarily, Captain Guy Briselden was awarded the Military Cross.

Objective Lead

At 0215 hours on the dark and dank morning of 26 February the QRL was retasked to attack Objective Lead some 30km east-south-east. The regiment began its Advance to Target at 0245 hours with 2 Troop of A Squadron QDG leading and at some 10km short of Zinc the squadrons moved into Advance to Contact formation. The objective was believed to be a battalion-sized position but there was little intelligence as to its occupants. The plan was to form a screen to the west of Lead with A Squadron QDG and B Squadron facing it while C and A Squadrons provided flank protection to the north and south respectively. The advance had been undertaken in pitch darkness and only feasible thanks to GPS. The regiment was ready by first light. Richard Quicke takes up the story:

At dawn it was misty with the poor visibility and at first no enemy could be seen in either vis [by eye] or thermal. The first contact was by a GW section who saw two tanks to the south, east of the QDGs. Called A Sqn QDG who said the tanks were friendly, so held fire. Ten minutes later an A-10 [Thunderbolt] strike destroyed one tank. The GW troop said what had happened so were given permission to fire. The time was now about 0700. The lased range to the targets was 4,090m. The first missile fired but could not be collected and it grounded. The second missile scored a

hit resulting in a kill. Ten more missiles were fired. Of the twelve fired, six malfunctioned. Of the six that functioned, four vehicle kills were recorded and two misses. There was no further movement in Lead, so through the FOO and RHQ, MLRS was called down onto the grid given by intel as containing an enemy tank company, although nothing could be seen. When MLRS came in there were several secondary explosions, and then a number of enemy vehicles appeared heading out of Lead in a NNE direction towards the US side of Phase Line Smash. Air was called in and two A-10s arrived, but the visibility was too poor for them to attack. More artillery could not be called in because some enemy were surrendering from their bunkers, some of whom were stretcher-case wounded. Therefore, GW and 1 Troop engaged the vehicles. The total kills were three T-55, two MTLB and two trucks. One of the T-55s was coming straight towards the troop and fired one shot from its main armament but did not hit anything. However, it was soon hit by a missile in the centre of its front and suffered an immediate kill. All three T-55 brewed, and those MTLB struck by missiles brewed as well but those hit by 30mm just stopped.

This missile was fired by Three Two Alpha at a tank but the control wire snapped after the maximum range of 4,100m so the missile went rogue, flying over the target but fortuitously hitting a fully laden truck some distance away causing its total destruction. To hit a target at maximum range under such awful weather conditions takes extraordinary skill and application. The failure rate of Swingfire in the Gulf was attributed to the vibration suffered by the stowed missiles over so many miles of travel inside the Strikers and MCTS Spartans.

Simultaneously, A Squadron QDG were heavily engaged in their attack on Objective Lead as the squadron commander Hamish Macdonald recounted:

At first light, 1 and 3 Troops identified dug-in armour to their front. At 0645 the bombardment started of Iraqi mechanised company and tank company positions with MLRS. This was followed by an airstrike by A-10 that knocked out three T-55 tanks, an MTLB and motor transport. A further bombardment ensued of another Iraqi tank company's position. By 0830 the leading troops were engaging the enemy with both 30mm cannon and anti-tank missiles while the Iraqis were responding. At one point squadron headquarters was engaged from the rear. There were reports from 2 Troop and the Advanced Alternative Headquarters of Scimitars withdrawing as Iraqi armour pushed north and north-east. Thinking that the Squadron had exposed flanks, I ordered a withdrawal, but was told by the commanding officer of the QRL to remain in position. In the meantime, 3 Troop engaged and destroyed an Iraqi T-55 tank and two personnel carriers. 2 Troop destroyed another MTLB.

While this was going on visibility had further deteriorated. Support Troop deployed its MSTAR and detected movement within Lead. This it engaged with four MLRS attacks. The squadron's guided weapons were used to destroy a further four personnel carriers as they tried to escape the barrage. In the rear of the squadron position, 2 Troop had destroyed two more personnel carriers and taken 40 prisoners. At 1145 A Squadron was ordered to withdraw after five hours of continuous action. However, 2 Troop remained firm covering a Scimitar with a thrown track and GW had a Striker with mechanical trouble. A vicious sandstorm had also blown up which further hampered the withdrawal. By 1400 replenishment was complete and all vehicles were again battle worthy.

To the south, C Squadron QRL was facing considerable difficulties as Iraqi tanks and AFVs attempted to escape Objective Platinum that was under attack from 7 Armoured Brigade. The Scimitar of Lieutenant Morley engaged the first T-55 at a distance of less than 1,500m but the sabot rounds just bounced off the turret. The Iraqi tank returned fire with its 12.7mm heavy machine gun striking the Scimitar in the lower hull. Two

rounds passed under the commander's seat, missing his legs by inches and lodged in the 30mm ammunition bins that began to smoulder and smoke. The crew immediately evacuated the vehicle but in his haste the driver, Trooper Wakelem, jumped to the ground, breaking his ankle. Lieutenant Horley recalled taking shelter 'behind the only bush in the desert' before the crew remounted their Scimitar. The vehicle continued unscathed until the end of the war. Unfortunately, two M-548 load carriers of C Squadron's echelon were not so lucky. One broke down and as the crew was being retrieved by the other M-548 it was pursued and engaged by the same T-55, killing two REME personnel. They were the only casualties suffered by the regiment during the war. Meanwhile, the squadron was warned that a column of Iraqi tanks was approaching from the west or, in other words, from the rear. The GW Troop from A Squadron was summoned to deal with the threat but the tanks passed in front of the Challengers of The Queen's Royal Irish Hussars and were completely destroyed. By midday the battle for Objective Lead was over.

The action on Objective Lead had been a significant success with the CVR(T) managing to acquire and engage depth targets with air and artillery fire while at the same time conducting a number of direct-fire engagements on enemy armour. In many respects the success of the action was the turning point in the overall operation. Prior to Lead there was every danger of concerted enemy intervention by the Iraqi tactical

BELOW A Scimitar of the Staffords Recce Group provides protection to M109A2 155mm howitzers and their M548 ammunition limbers as the guns redeploy to new firing positions in support of the Staffords Battle Group. The ready availability of immediate fire support from the Royal Artillery was one of the defining successes in all the contact battles of the war.

reserves; after Lead the chances of a counter-attack were minimal. In the words of the CRA, Major General Ian Drurie:

> By the end of that marvellous action which so well justified the GOC's approach to the Depth Battle, it was evident that the enemy was not going to move to us at all and we could take more risks in speeding up the Contact Battle and there was not much to be gained in trying to push 16/5th Lancers on again into the depth.

As the QRL and QDG withdrew westwards towards Zinc, 7th Armoured Brigade launched its attack on Objective Platinum. The Staffords Battle Group crossed their start line at the H-Hour of 1245 hours. At the same time,

BELOW A MILAN ATGW missile is loaded on to the Spartan MCT or MILAN Compact Turret of Four One Delta during live-fire training at the Devil Dog Dragoon Range in December 1990. During their initial training at Hohne, the MILAN Platoon of the Staffords fired a total of 288 missiles in two days – more than was used during the whole of Operation Desert Sabre. The MCT(S) carries 12 reload missiles in the hull but more were commonly crammed inside the rear compartment. The reloading procedure was not ideal in combat conditions with crew members fully exposed to enemy fire.

the Reconnaissance Group, comprising the Reconnaissance Platoon and the Mobile MILAN Section, was manoeuvring to protect the eastern flank of the battle group as it advanced south. Captain Richard Wootton recalled:

> We were now heading due south and providing flank protection to the east. Sgt Dawson's and C/Sgt Cronin's sections moved off early in an attempt to catch up with the remainder of the battle group. When the remainder of the recce group moved off, they spotted what appeared to be an Iraqi HQ position about 1,500m to the east. The two T-55s on the position were manned but fortunately we were to the rear of their arcs. Corporal Tyler in C/S 21A engaged one of them and C/Sgt Banks in C/S 22 the other. Despite first round hits in both cases and subsequent hits by L/Cpl McGarry in 21A, the effect on the T-55s was solely to force the commanders to batten down. Meanwhile Pte Grainger, Sgt Thomas's operator in 41C, and Cpl Fern, the commander of 41C who explained to his operator that he hadn't been in MILAN for this length of time to miss the opportunity to fire for real as he took the firing post controls, prepared to engage then pressed the button. Both scored direct hits and lifted the turrets off the hulls. Private Grainger then went on to destroy a ZSU-23-4, an MTLB and a command bunker, which had had a couple of sandbags dislodged by 21A's 30mm. The remaining Scimitars engaged the soft-skinned vehicles on the position, including a fuel tanker, with both 30mm and 7.62mm. The exception was Corporal Jackson, who provided harassing 30mm fire all over the position!

The commander of MCTS Four One Delta was Corporal Darren Fern:

> I first saw a BMP which was out of view of the rest of the recce group. It had moved from its scrape and it looked as if it was going to engage us. I was screaming at Morris in the back 'Take that vehicle out!' But he was having problems locating it through his sights. It was getting a bit dangerous, so I got in the back and I hit the

RIGHT With the famous Bulls Head insignia of the Second World War 79th Armoured Division on the back bin, a Spartan of 31st Armoured Field Squadron accompanies the specialised armour of the Route Development Group during the advance into Kuwait. In the background are a variety of Royal Engineer AFVs including Chieftain AVLB and AVRE as well as the venerable Centurion 165mm AVRE.

BMP. It just obliterated it. The turret came off and the doors and hatches blew open from the pressure of the round. At this point, I switched straight away to my right-hand missile and fired at the T-55. As the missile was flying, I saw the tank commander's hatch open and he came out waving a piece of white cloth. But it was too late then, and the missile hit the turret at the rear. He came flying out and then the turret lifted off, and then all the ammunition blew up.

By now, the Iraqi high command was paralysed while the common soldier was surrendering in droves. On the eastern sector between the coast and the Wadi Al-Batin, the Iraqi front had collapsed and coalition

BELOW The expectation of a significant number of casualties due to chemical and biological weapons led to a large expansion of the medical services within all formations and units. The Regimental Aid Post of the 16/5th QRL had an additional Sultan and six Samaritans, whereas armoured and infantry formations still employed the FV432 ambulance. This Samaritan of A Squadron QDG is liberally adorned with international red crosses and flies the Y Ddraig Goch for mutual recognition, although it was somewhat optimistic to expect an A-10 pilot to recognise the Welsh Dragon as friendly.

ABOVE The CVR(T)s of the Recce Group of the Fusiliers Battle Group fought a decisive action on the night of 26 February against entrenched Iraqi troops defending an oil pumping station standing alone in the wide expanse of the desert. Unlike Challenger and Warrior, CVR(T) had only limited night vision capability so improvisation was the order of the day through a combination of GPS, OTIS, Spyglass and the MIRA thermal sight of Spartan MCT(S) together with considerable firepower of the CVR(T)s themselves and supporting artillery.

forces were in the outskirts of Kuwait City. In the west, XVIII US Corps had reached the Euphrates Valley while VII US Corps was poised to destroy the three mobile divisions of the Republican Guard during the night of 26/27 February. On its right flank, 1st UK Armoured Division launched a coordinated assault by 4th Armoured Brigade against Objective Tungsten.

The Battle of the Pipeline

On the afternoon of 26 February, the Fusiliers Battle Group had cleared Objectives Brass and Steel and was replenishing its vehicles when disaster struck. Two Warrior IFVs were hit by Maverick missiles fired by an A-10 Thunderbolt close-air support aircraft. Some 9 soldiers were killed and another 11 wounded. It was an awful shock but the Fusiliers had little time to dwell on the tragedy since the next phase of the operation, the advance to Objective Tungsten, was due to start that evening. Supported by D Squadron of the 14th/20th Hussars, the Reconnaissance Group led the 4th Brigade against an extensive

Iraqi position where the enemy put up greater opposition than previously encountered. The battle for Objective Tungsten lasted most of the night with the Reconnaissance Group to the fore as Captain Paul Nanson recounted:

As we began the advance MLRS began to fire over our heads onto Tungsten some kilometres in front. It was a clear night and the visibility was good, a welcome change from the previous evening's advance towards Brass. My gunner, Lance Corporal Bruton, kept the platoon on course with the GPS whilst I observed the desert with the OTIS mounted on top of the Scimitar. About an hour into the advance, Sergeant Oliver's section, which had pushed forward some distance, reported a sighting of vehicles to their front. I brought them to a halt and the MILAN section moved forward to observe the target with MIRA.

From a distance the target did indeed look like a gathering of vehicles. The skyline was broken by what appeared to be large antennas. Conscious of the risk of fratricide, I broke silence on the command net and asked the CO to confirm that there were no friendly in front of us. He confirmed that there was only the Royal Scots on our left flank and were some distance behind. I tasked Sergeant Oliver to move forward and investigate. From the map, the contact appeared to be on or around the pipeline. I allowed Oliver to continue as I manoeuvred the remainder of the group around the area of the crossing. Sergeant Rudsdale had a good idea of the location of the crossing and was keen to get on with the marking before the rest of the battle group arrived. It was as we moved that Sergeant Oliver's section reported a contact and commenced engaging with HE and machine gun. The full report described a bunker complex around a series of buildings overlooking the pipeline. There was nothing on the map and so I assumed it must be some sort of pumping station, located at the crossing site. This was the only crossing for miles and it seemed as though we would have no option but to fight. As contact reports started coming in from the other sections I sent my own contact report to BG HQ. Movement of men, vehicles and a report of a large-barrelled weapon of some sort prompted me to engage using the whole platoon.

With considerable skill, Colour Sergeant McCarthy's section escorted the Royal Engineer Spartan reconnaissance vehicles forward in the complete darkness. A couple of suitable crossing points for the battle group were found over the pipeline which was some 3m off the desert floor. These were improved and strengthened by Lieutenant Mike Lobb's Sappers of 3 Troop to provide a sand rampart capable of bearing the 70 tonnes of

THIS PAGE The Scimitar, Callsign Two Three Alpha, is shown before, during and after the ground offensive of Operation Desert Sabre. The name MARTINIQUE, despite the curious spelling, indicates this Scimitar is from the Reconnaissance Platoon of 3RD Battalion, Royal Regiment of Fusiliers (3RRF) as all their AFVs were named after Regimental Battle Honours. The Scottish flags signify the provenance of the crew as 1st Battalion Queen's Royal Highlanders that were attached to 3RRF with Corporal Derrick McManus enjoying a mug of tea in the turret after the end of hostilities. Two Three Alpha was part of the first ground action of the Fusiliers Battle Group on Objective Copper South on 26 February 1991.
(Derrick McManus)

a Challenger MBT. Once across, the Fusiliers Battle Group had to turn northwards to the start line before Objective Tungsten but it took a significant time for all of its vehicles to negotiate the two crossing sites.

Meanwhile, the Reconnaissance Platoon had observed some buildings beside the pipeline with numerous Iraqi soldiers moving about, so their vehicles formed up in line abreast and engaged the area with coaxial machine gun and cannon fire. The enemy returned fire and tried to manoeuvre an artillery piece into position near to the gate of the oil installation. This movement was observed by Corporal Dave Weaver in Four Two Charlie, who immediately destroyed it with a MILAN

missile. Similarly, Callsign Four Four Charlie acquired a heat source of a large body of men congregating inside the doorway of a building. Each time the door opened, the heat signature became clearer as the people inside were exposed to the MIRA sight. Corporal Geoff Green ordered his gunner, Fusilier Dale Trantor, to engage and, at a range of only 500m, the building disintegrated under the impact of the missile from the MCTS, which the crew had christened 'Appetite for Destruction'.

Captain Nanson continued:

On the command net, the CO ordered the tanks forward in support and the mortar platoon reported that they were in position to provide indirect fire. There was by now limited small-arms fire coming from the enemy and a further two MILAN missiles had reduced the activity around the bunkers. Sergeant Oliver's section was now only 200m from the complex and so, much to the disappointment of the mortars, I decided that we were too close for a fire mission. The engineers continued to mark the crossing and very soon Corporal Haley in Callsign Two Four Alpha reported white flags in the vicinity of the bunker complex. Colour Sergeant McCarthy and Two Three crossed and covered the remainder of the platoon across. Prisoners were left for the RSM and the Reconnaissance Group continued onto the FUP. There were still a number of heat sources to our front and it was a relief to hear the tanks of B Squadron moving up to take over the engagement.

RIGHT AND CENTRE On the morning of Wednesday 27 February at 1119 hours an unfortunate 'blue on blue' incident occurred when two Scorpions, 'ROCHESTER' and 'RAPHOE' of the QRIH Reconnaissance Troop, were struck by coaxial and main armament rounds from an M1A1 Abrams of 2nd Armored Cavalry Regiment. 'ROCHESTER (bottom) suffered severe damage while 'RAPHOE' (top) was struck through the rear turret bin. Fortunately, casualties were light with Lance Corporals Bamforth and Lynch injured. *(QRIH)*

The firefight had lasted for almost an hour and towards the end the tanks of B Squadron arrived. Its squadron leader, Major Richard Shirreff, inquired of TAC HQ: 'Now that we are in contact do you want us to take over or for your less-well-protected callsigns to continue?' The battle of the pipeline was over. It was the last significant CVR(T) action of the Gulf War.

Even so, the campaign continued unabated and on the morning of Wednesday 27 February at 1119 hours an unfortunate 'blue on blue' incident occurred when two Scorpions, ROCHESTER and RAPHOE, of the Queen's Royal Irish Hussars Reconnaissance Troop were struck by coaxial and main armament rounds from an M1 Abrams of 2 Armored Cavalry Regiment. Despite severe damage to

LEFT 02FF09, the Spartan of Lieutenant Nick Fenton, commanding Support Troop, A Squadron, QDG, churns up the desert in the final dash for the Basra–Kuwait highway in the closing hours of Operation Desert Sabre. Like many AFVs during the land campaign, this Spartan carries a roll of CARM (or Chemical Agent Resistant Material) as part of the overall NBC protection measures. *(Robin Watt)*

the vehicles, casualties were light with Lance Corporals Bamforth and Lynch injured. By now, the 16th/5th Queen's Royal Lancers had been redeployed from the Depth Fire Group to provide security for the Divisional Administrative Area (DAA) with its hundreds of soft-skinned vehicles struggling to catch up with the teeth arms now advancing rapidly into Kuwait. The DAA was perceived to be vulnerable to Iraqi stragglers or diehard Ba'athist elements, so the QRL were obliged to retrace their tracks to undertake this important task.

At the same time, A Squadron of The Queen's Dragoon Guards was returned to 7th Armoured Brigade to provide their reconnaissance screen for the advance into Kuwait. At 0730 on 27 February, the squadron, covered by attack helicopters, led the rapid advance to Objective Varsity. On the final day of the war, A Squadron, 1st The Queen's Dragoon Guards, closely followed by the tanks of The Queen's Royal Irish Hussars, set out for Objective Cobalt astride the main road from Kuwait City to Basra, arriving at 0800 hours just as President Bush declared a ceasefire. The 100 Hours War was over. The date of 1 March was St David's Day and fittingly the Welsh Dragon flew from every QDG CVR(T) vehicle. Fortunately, the squadron did not suffer a single casualty during the land campaign. On the other hand, Iraq lost some 25,000 killed and scores of thousands wounded; 3,008 of 3,600 tanks; 2,140 of 3,200 artillery guns; 1,857 of 3,950 APCs as well as some 25% of its combat aircraft. Saddam Hussein's vainglorious 'mother of all battles' ended in ignominy and the bloodshed of many reluctant martyrs. The UN and Coalition Forces' response was overwhelming and Kuwait was liberated. In the words of Thomas Jefferson: 'From time to time, the tree of liberty must be watered with the blood of tyrants and patriots.'

Postscript

On the evening of Thursday 7 March, Major Hamish Macdonald, commander of A Squadron, QDG, was in his tent writing his after-battle report when he was joined by a jerboa – the original Desert Rat. It sat on an open patch of sand grooming its cream and ginger fur with its large eyes glistening in the light of a gas lamp before munching contentedly on compo biscuits through the night. For the Desert Rats of 4th and 7th Armoured Brigades, it was a fitting end to Operation Desert Sabre. The 1st Armoured Division advanced 290km in 66 hours; destroyed three Iraqi divisions; took 7,024 prisoners (including two divisional commanders) and captured over 400 pieces of equipment and 2,000 small arms. Also taken were 50 T-55s; 61 T-59s; 13 T-62s; 104 other A Vehicles; 9 missile systems; 69 B Vehicles and 242 artillery/AA weapons. It was a famous victory by any standard.

Operation Telic, 2003 – The Garden of Eden

In January 2003, British armed forces were deployed to Kuwait in support of the US-led coalition to invade Iraq and topple the Ba'athist regime of Saddam Hussein. The land forces comprised 1st Armoured Division with 7 Armoured Brigade, 16 Air Assault Brigade and 3 Royal Marines Commando Brigade. In a remarkable operation of logistics, all fighting units were in country and fit for battle within ten weeks. The division included 6,500 vehicles with 1,037 AFVs, of which there were 155 CVR(T)s and 6 Stormer minelaying vehicles. The CVR(T)s were employed by 1st The Queen's Dragoon Guards and D Squadron, Household Cavalry Regiment (HCR). As the Formation Reconnaissance Regiment, A Squadron of 1 QDG was attached to 7 Armoured Brigade, B Squadron was employed as divisional troops while C Squadron was attached to 3 Commando Brigade. D Squadron, HCR, was attached to 16 Air Assault Brigade.

Hostilities began on 20 March 2003 with 'decapitation' air strikes against the Iraqi high command and leadership with the main phase of the air campaign beginning the next day.

Initially, D Squadron, HCR, provided protection for Royal Engineers breaching the massive sand berm along the border with Iraq. Thereafter, the squadron moved north to mark a route through the Rumailah oilfields for the 5th Marines. After a swift advance into Iraq, the momentum faltered

as a number of options were considered for the next phase of the operations. A northern alternative was to exploit deep over the Al Hammar canal and interdict enemy forces moving along the Euphrates river and Highway 6, while the southern option was for 1 PARA to air assault the Qalat Salah airfield with D Squadron screening the advance of the Marine Expeditionary Force against the Iraqi 10th Armoured Division to the west. In the meantime, the squadron despatched flying columns to assist other battle groups.

Major Richard Taylor of The Life Guards was in command of D Squadron, HCR, and recounts their part in Operation Telic:

The northern option finally got the go ahead on 26 March. I felt a bit like Michael Caine in A Bridge Too Far when XXX Corps was poised along a levee [embankment] waiting to advance north into Holland. The squadron were now strung along a levee in the dark waiting to push north over the Al Hammar canal and break out of a bridgehead created by 3 PARA – the anticipation was electric as this was our

first major advance into Iraqi-held territory with 16 Air Assault Brigade. The plan was to scout north-east, where the Iraqi 6 Armoured Division least expected us to advance, until we were in a position to interdict Highway 6 – the main route from Baghdad to Basra, which ran along the Shatt-al-Arab and over the junction of the Euphrates and Tigris rivers, the historic 'Garden of Eden'. This would deny the Iraqis the ability to engage the Rumailah oilfields with their III Corps artillery and would ultimately neutralise three Iraqi Divisions (6 Armoured, 14 and 18) in keeping the route to Basra open.

As first light appeared on 27 March, Lieutenant A.K. MacEwen's, 2 Troop led over the Al Hammar canal – not a canal by British standards as it is over a kilometre wide! There was a flurry of excitement as 2 Troop was tasked to probe forward in the dense fog to identify a T-55 spotted by 3 PARA. Captain Chris Morgan – the FOO – was under immense pressure from the Battery Commander to push to the front and adjust artillery fire onto it but

ABOVE A Scimitar of D Squadron, HCR, works in conjunction with a USMC AAVP-7A1 amphibious assault vehicle during the initial stages of Operation Telic.

visibility was down to 400m and the Paras were all around the target area. Luckily my obstinacy in holding him back was justified when 2 Troop reported that the 'T-55' was a drainpipe sticking out of a berm!

Pushing ahead of 3 PARA, we passed a number of abandoned Iraqi artillery and tank positions and cleared 17km ahead to a holding area on the edge of a large irrigation ditch. There we spent a very surreal day in the sun waiting for the guns to push forward to cover our next bound. The ground ahead was drained marshland intersected by deep irrigation ditches and dusty tracks on large 15ft levees.

The afternoon was spent motorbike watching. We quickly established that no one with any sense would be driving around an area of dangerous irrigation ditches close to Coalition forces without malicious intent. They were in fact armed artillery observers in civilian clothes working to a number of FOOs in pick-up trucks and using Motorola UHF comms to call for fire. Initially brigade orders were to try to make them surrender. This worked for LCoH Stokoe and CoH Matthews who took three EPWs [enemy prisoners of war] in the south – but 1 Troop were a bit perplexed when they were told that they had to capture a motorcyclist who was 'dicking' them 2km away over a 5ft wide irrigation ditch.

Finally at 0500 hours on 28 March, the 7 Royal Horse Artillery guns moved in range. We advanced as we had practised at CATT [Combined Arms Tactical Trainer] and on numerous occasions in the Kuwaiti desert with direct support from 3AAC. Lieutenant A.D. Tweedie's 3 Troop led the advance north with Captain C.J.L. White's MSG in echelon. LCoH Goodwin had the first sighting of two white civilian pick-ups, which we knew from the previous day to be Iraqi FOO parties. The Squadron continued the advance and Lieutenant C.J.L. Speers' 1 Troop were tasked with outflanking and stopping the pick-ups. Shortly afterwards LCoH Goodwin received the first of many incoming artillery 50m to his left – this had to be identified by CoH Simpson as he could not hear it through his ANR headset!

Blue on Blue

Major Richard Taylor continues the account:

By 1015 hours the Squadron had advanced a total of 44km from the Bde Main Body, destroyed a company location of BMPs and mortars with direct fire and close air support (CAS) and had gained eyes on Highway 6 and the date palms of 'The Garden of Eden'. The Brigade COS was delighted and the squadron moved to consolidate along a levee nicknamed Route Spear. In the process LCoH Goodwin had been admonished by his Gunner Tpr Tansey for attempting to video an engagement with a BMP. At the same time 1 Troop finally trapped the enemy FOOs and tried to get them to surrender. The response was a courageous counterattack by five enemy pick-ups firing rocket-propelled grenades and small arms. As Lieutenant C.J.L. Speers destroyed the first pick-up with 30mm, he left the pressel down on his radio so that the squadron could hear the automatic fire and whoops of 'target'. Thirty minutes later all five pick-ups had been destroyed – CoH Heaton destroyed one with Swingfire at great cost to the taxpayer! LCoH Brooks dismounted and took 14 prisoners of war. Later that afternoon 2 Troop were patrolling up the west side of Route Spear, when they were engaged out of the blue by two American A-10 aircraft.

While the unit was pushing forward about 25 miles north of Basra, scouting for elements of the Iraqi 6th Armoured Division on 28 March, it was attacked by an American A10 tank-buster aircraft. Trooper Finney recalls: 'I was driving a Scimitar on Route Spear next to the Shatt al-Arab waterway 40km north of Basra. We were running parallel to a small village when we were hit on top. I didn't know what had happened – I thought we were under attack from a rocket-propelled grenade.' In fact, his Scimitar had been hit and set on fire by 30mm cannon shells from two American A-10 Warthogs. Ammunition began to explode in the turret: 'The commander got out and the gunner, LCoH Al Tudball, was wounded. I started to reverse but backed into the Scimitar behind, which had also been hit.' Trooper Finney found cover but climbed back into the burning Scimitar to rescue the gunner. 'I could see that Al Tudball was trapped half out of his hatch so I got him on to the ground and started first aid. His headset was hanging off the side of the turret so I used it to send a report.' Trooper Finney took the wounded gunner to a Royal Engineers Spartan recce vehicle, which had moved up to help as the A-10s began another attack. Both men received fragmentation wounds.

Sergeant Andrew Sindall, from 23 Engineer Regiment (Air Assault), provided first aid and threw red smoke to signal to the A-10s that they were attacking friendly vehicles. But he could not stop the second attack, during which he was wounded and his Spartan hit. He carried on helping the Scimitar crewmen and got them into the back of his vehicle. Trooper Finney turned to the second Scimitar to help. 'LCoH Matty Hull, their gunner, was still stuck in the turret. There were engineers already trying to get him out.' He was beaten back by the heat, smoke and fumes and Hull died of his wounds. Finney, who collapsed and was recovered by Spartan crew, was not the only hero of the A-10 incident.

Lance Corporal of Horse Jonathan Woodgate was the driver of one of the other Scimitars struck by 30mm Gatling-gun fire:

The first thing I knew when we actually got hit was the wagon just stopped dead and sparks came round flying over my shoulders. I wasn't quite sure what had happened so I checked over my shoulder. The whole thing was full of smoke and then flames. You know it just lit up. I thought at first that we had been ambushed. We were in that part where the Iraqi 6th Army Brigade was in so I thought it would be them that smashed us in. Then I just tried to get out. The driver's hatch jammed so I had to struggle about with that for quite a while. I was pretty shocked as I was only 19 years old. It became pretty evident what was going on. The A-10s came on their second swoop. They were pretty low. The

whole end of the back of the vehicle was ripped open and the turret had been blown off. If you stood in front of it you could see out of the back of it. Tragically after the first run LCoH Hull was killed and LCpl Tudball, LCoH Gerrard and Lieutenant A.K. MacEwen were injured. Tpr Finney dragged LCpl Tudball out of the turret, placed him in safety and bandaged his wounds. He then went back to the vehicle to send a sitrep on the casualties, as smoke was obscuring the entire scene. Simultaneously Sgt Sindall, one of the attached Engineer Recce Sergeants, ordered his vehicle forward to the Scimitars to pick up the wounded. Just as Finney was carrying Tudball towards the Spartan the second A-10 run came in injuring Finney, Tudball again and Sindall. Wounded, Sindall dismounted, assessed the situation and called forward his other vehicle. He then threw all his red smoke and recovered the injured. At this point Sindall, Finney and some others tried to climb onto the rear Scimitar to rescue Hull, but were beaten back by the intense heat, smoke and ammunition cooking off. They therefore recovered a bound behind, where Captain Hooper, LSgt Jolley and LSgt Whitley attended to the wounded. Having persuaded the RAF that the HLS [Helicopter Landing Site] was 'almost' safe, they were casevaced to the hospital ship Argus. Trooper Finney was awarded the George Cross for his acts of heroism.

At exactly the same time as the Friendly Fire incident, LCoH Flynn sighted two T-55s, a BMP and a D-30 howitzer. Only his Scimitar and LCoH Telling's Striker were in position to fight off the Iraqi armour from threatening the casevac 4km away. Under artillery fire themselves, SHQ tasked Flynn and Telling to prevent the armour from interfering with the casevac. Coming under intense tank and artillery fire, Telling withdrew to set up a separated sight position for his Swingfire. For 30min Flynn endured accurate artillery and tank fire and suppressed the Iraqi armour with 140 rounds of 30mm to protect the extraction of casualties. Telling then destroyed the first T-55 and Flynn's firing forced the second

Chapter Six

CVR(T) upgrades

Over the years CVR(T) underwent a life extension programme to meet the needs of the contemporary battlefield, with a dependable diesel engine and much enhanced sighting systems for night-fighting. Several new variants were introduced to expand the capabilities of the CVR(T) family, particularly for air defence and export sales.

OPPOSITE The CVR(T) family entered service in 1972 and, with the Life Extension Programme of the late 1990s, it continues to perform as an effective AFV in armies across the world even after 50 years.

The last CVR(T) vehicle in a total of 1,863 for the UK Ministry of Defence was delivered in 1986 with a breakdown by type as follows:

Scorpion	313
Striker	89
Spartan	691
Samaritan	50
Sultan	291
Samson	95
Scimitar	334

The CVR(T) family had proved successful in service but technology moves on and various failings were coming to the fore. Primarily, the night sights had inadequate range for both detection and identification: a fundamental deficiency in a reconnaissance AFV. Range estimation for gunnery was still down to the 'Mark 1 Eyeball' of the turret crew with on average 25% inaccuracy rate. The manual turret traverse hampered target acquisition and fine laying during an engagement while adding to crew fatigue. These factors considerably reduced the chance of a first-round hit. Furthermore, the firepower of the L23 76mm gun was now woefully inadequate against Warsaw Pact AFVs, particularly when firing at a target head-on. Automotively, the Jaguar J60 engine had not proved to be as robust as expected with engine life approximately 8,000 miles as against 10,000 miles of the original GSR. Similarly, the tracks were not sufficiently durable and required frequent inspection and maintenance. By now, the CVR(T) family was the last user of petrol within the AFV fleet, while all variants, being front-engined, suffered from a high thermal signature, making detection and identification by IR or thermal imaging sights too easy.

In response to these problems, a CVR(T) Mid-Life Improvement Programme was initiated by the Operational Requirements Committee (ORC) in May 1978 in response to GST 3762 of 15 June 1977. The three aspects of firepower, mobility and survivability were addressed but in all considerations cost constraints were to prevail since any modification programme had to be funded from outside the Post Design Service budget.

Accordingly, the upgunning of Scorpion was never a serious proposition although the addition of an ATGW launcher on the turret side was considered.

Similarly, there was to be no replacement of the Jaguar J60 with limited mechanical improvements being of a minor nature, such as the installation of electronic ignition for the J60 engine. The most important area for improvement was deemed to be an increase in surveillance capability with the fitting of TI sights for both commander and gunner by using components of the UK TI Common Module Programme.

Other improvements under active consideration were the provision of a laser rangefinder, power elevation and traverse of the turret and a thermal pointer as a lower-cost alternative to full TI. The first report on the feasibility study by Director General Fighting Vehicles Establishment (DGFVE) was presented on 5 February 1979 but any decision as to implementation was delayed as a series of major parallel AFV studies were concurrently under consideration by the ORC. In the event, the Mid-Life Improvement Programme withered on the vine and further developments of CVR(T) were undertaken by Alvis and other private companies such as Perkins, Avimo, Barr and Stroud and so on.

Stretched Spartan – FV4333

From the outset the MoD realised the main drawback of the FV103 Spartan APC was its lack of space for both crew and equipment. Once the initial trials of CVR(T) were completed, Prototype 11 was modified at MVEE with an extra wheel station per side to test the concept of an extended Spartan and indeed the whole FV100 series. However, the appearance of the BMP Infantry Fighting Vehicle (IFV) at the 7 November 1967 Victory Parade in Moscow galvanised NATO powers into finding a counter to such a radical AFV that had entered service with the 120th Guards 'Rogachev' Motor Rifle Division the year before. In the same year, FVRDE began concept studies of a comparable IFV. Meanwhile, the British Army first responded

to the new Soviet threat by fitting a Rarden 30mm-armed Fox turret atop an FV432 APC.

Several concepts were pursued for an IFV with three weight classes envisaged: Light at 14.6 tonnes, Medium at 24.2 tonnes and an uparmoured version of the Medium that weighed 28.9 tonnes with the designation of Mechanised Infantry Combat Vehicle (MICV). An even heavier version incorporating the revolutionary new composite armour developed under Project Burlington, later Chobham armour, was proposed but this was soon discarded on the grounds of cost. In 1970, outline feasibility studies were undertaken at FVRDE for what was now known as 'Stretched Spartan' incorporating an enlarged box body with the following particular roles:

1. A command post/Royal Signals vehicle.
2. A fitters' vehicle for battlefield repair.
3. Light 10-man APC within the MICV programme.

A mobile test rig was produced at FVRDE within three months by combining the hulls of two badly damaged Spartans. At the outset, it was fitted with the standard Jaguar J60 engine but this proved underpowered for a vehicle weighted to 14 tons. It was proposed to use the same Rolls-Royce C6TFR engine as the Combat Engineer Tractor (CET) then under development. However, the concept of three classes of MICV fell by the wayside to become MCV80 that finally emerged as the FV510 Warrior Infantry Fighting Vehicle (IFV) in November 1984. Development continued of a vehicle with a battle weight of 8.75 tons (19,000lb) so that the existing Jaguar J60 engine could be utilised with a power-to-weight ratio of 22bhp per ton. This was intended to cost no more than £50,000 so as to be attractive to foreign customers and a cheaper alternative to a fully-fledged IFV.

Coincidentally, the Belgian Liaison Officer on the CVR(T) Project Team indicated there was a potential requirement for a light, ten-man APC for the Belgian Army with the added attraction of sharing many components with their existing CVR(T) fleet. In addition, a market sales survey suggested that worldwide sales could be considerable. There was also the possibility of a British Army requirement for some 200 of such a vehicle to replace certain variants of the FV430 series. In a letter to the Assistant Chief of the General Staff (Operational Requirements) dated 30 October 1974, the DGFVE requested that a final decision on stretched Spartan be made

as the Belgians wished to know by the end of the year. There was also the delicate matter of whether to include the new variant within the existing Memorandum of Understanding with Belgium or else pass the design concept to Alvis as a private venture given that development costs to that point had amounted to £1.2million.

A purpose-built version of stretched Spartan was manufactured by ROF Leeds and was first shown in public at the British Army Equipment Exhibition in June 1978 under the designation FV4333. Of note, the vehicle was the first CVR(T) variant to incorporate a Perkins diesel engine in place of the Jaguar J60 petrol type.

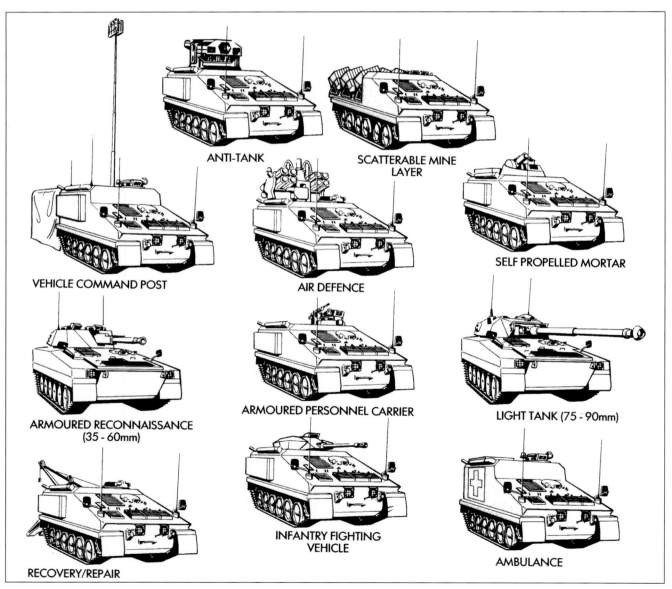

ANTI-TANK

SCATTERABLE MINE LAYER

VEHICLE COMMAND POST

AIR DEFENCE

SELF PROPELLED MORTAR

ARMOURED RECONNAISSANCE (35 - 60mm)

ARMOURED PERSONNEL CARRIER

LIGHT TANK (75 - 90mm)

RECOVERY/REPAIR

INFANTRY FIGHTING VEHICLE

AMBULANCE

When foreign sales did not materialise, the design concept and marketing rights were sold to Alvis in 1980, the parent company of the CVR(T) family. After further development, the APC was named Stormer in July 1981. Production began in 1982 with the first deliveries of 25 Stormers and 25 Scorpion 90s for the Malaysian Army in 1983.

Spartan MCT

The Spartan APC proved to be a highly capable platform for carrying various weapon systems. Once Scimitar became integral to the reconnaissance platoons of infantry mechanised battalions, it was logical to enhance the anti-tank capability of such formations with an ATGW system similar to the Scorpion and Striker combination. The weapon selected was the Euromissile MILAN man portable missile that was also employed by infantry anti-tank platoons. Mounted on the roof of Spartan, the MILAN Compact Turret (MCT) accommodated all the equipment required to fire the missile from under armour with an effective range out to 2,000m. The MCT mounted two firing tubes and the crew had the option either to fire from inside the vehicle or deploy from it and use a standard infantry firing post. A further 12 MILAN missile reloads were

LEFT The Stormer Tactical Reconnaissance Vehicle (TRV) is the companion variant to the Stormer HVM SP. Ten TRVs were procured and their role is to reconnoitre suitable firing sites and act as missile replenishment vehicles. This TRV is leading a parade of 12 Regiment Royal Artillery.

Sabre reconnaissance vehicle

Following the demise of Scorpion and the inadequacy of Fox within the British Army, a logical CVR(T) development was a vehicle combining the hulls of redundant Scorpions with the turrets of the Fox. Continuing the 'S'-themed naming tradition of the CVR(T) family, the new reconnaissance vehicle was called Sabre. It was accepted for service with the British Army in August 1993. The Royal Ordnance 30mm Rarden cannon of Sabre is the same as that for Scimitar, so logistical support and crew training are much simplified. However, the original L37A2 7.62mm machine gun has been replaced by the Boeing Company L94A1 7.62mm Chain Gun as fitted to the Warrior IFV and Challenger 2 MBT. Other modifications include a turret adaptor collar; additional stowage boxes around the hull and turret sides; a new gun crutch for improved driver's vision; new 66mm smoke dischargers; and domed hatches for both commander and gunner for greater comfort inside the turret. Alvis supplied the MoD with 138 conversion kits and the work was undertaken by the ABRO (Army Base Repair Organisation) facility at Donnington. The first

ABOVE The Spartan MILAN Mobile Compact Turret was also known as MCT(S) for short. Four One Delta was as MCT(S) of the 1 STAFFORDS Mobile MILAN Platoon commanded by Corporal Darren 'Eddy' Fern. This vehicle nicknamed 'TANK BUSTERS' scored a notable success on 26 February 1991 when it destroyed a BMP and a T-55 with a 'left and right' – one hit with each missile.

RIGHT The Sabre reconnaissance vehicle was the marriage of a Fox turret and a Scorpion hull once both vehicles had been withdrawn from service. This is the Sabre S2 reference vehicle at the Alvis works in Coventry.

carried inside the hull. The 75 Spartan MCTs were converted at 23 Base Workshops REME in Wetter, Germany, with the first delivery to the British Army in September 1986. The MCT proved highly effective during the Gulf War of 1991 and ended its career as the Sturgeon OPFOR vehicle at BATUS.

vehicles were completed in 1994 and Sabres were issued to TA Yeomanry reconnaissance regiments and the reconnaissance platoons of mechanised infantry battalions. The Sabre was withdrawn from service in 2004 following the decision not to upgrade the vehicle with diesel engines as for the rest of the CVR(T) fleet.

Scorpion 90

The limitations of the L23 76mm gun of Scorpion became apparent with the introduction of new armour arrays in the 1980s. As prime contractor for CVR(T), Alvis addressed the issue by mounting a 90mm

six-cylinder T6.3544 turbocharged diesel engine, the vehicle had a power-to-weight ratio of 22.44bhp/ton (16.44 kW/tonne) giving a top speed of 45mph (72.5kph). Designated Scorpion 90, Alvis offered the vehicle on the international market in 1980. Foreign customers include Indonesia, Malaysia, Nigeria and Venezuela. The British Army purchased a single example of Scorpion 90 for trials purposes but upgunning of the Scorpion was never really a serious consideration because of the limited number of main armament rounds carried. It also did not wish to compromise the manufacture of 76mm ammunition at the ROFs for existing foreign customers.

ABOVE One example of Scorpion 90 was acquired by the British Army for trials purposes.

Cockerill Mark 3 rifled gun firing fin-stabilised ammunition. With a maximum range of 4,000m, the Cockerill gun was manufactured by the Belgian company CMI Defense and provided a powerful main armament on lightweight AFVs. It fired six natures of ammunition: APFSDS-T, HE-T, HEAT-T, Smoke-WP-T, HESH-T and Canister, as well as practice and drill rounds. The gun was mounted in the Scorpion turret designated AC90 with an electrical power traverse and elevation system rather than the manual controls of the original Scorpion. Powered by the Perkins

Streaker HMLC

Late in 1982, Alvis completed the prototype of a High Mobility Load Carrier (HMLC) as a private venture in response to an MoD requirement for a Barmine Layer Tractor and to replace the company's Stalwart 6×6 HMLC. The vehicle was based on the chassis of the Spartan APC. It was powered by the standard 4.2-litre petrol engine or by the Perkins T6.3544 200bhp turbocharged diesel coupled to an automatic transmission. Maximum road speed was 84kph, road range 480km, the unloaded weight was

RIGHT The Streaker HMLC was originally designed as a Barmine Layer Tractor that spawned a whole family of versatile AFVs.

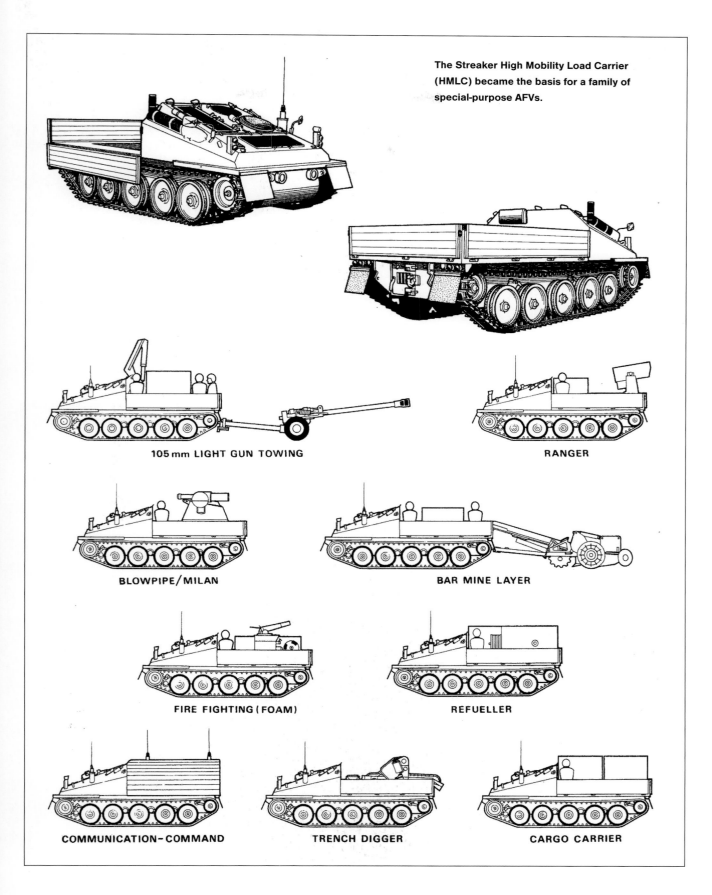

The Streaker High Mobility Load Carrier (HMLC) became the basis for a family of special-purpose AFVs.

105 mm LIGHT GUN TOWING

RANGER

BLOWPIPE/MILAN

BAR MINE LAYER

FIRE FIGHTING (FOAM)

REFUELLER

COMMUNICATION–COMMAND

TRENCH DIGGER

CARGO CARRIER

ABOVE AND LEFT A version of the Streaker HMLC was fitted with an LAU97 FZ 70mm 40-round rocket launcher for trials purposes but, proving that there is nothing new under the sun, one of the original concepts for the Lightweight High Mobility Tracked Vehicle family was a multiple rocket launcher that was to become reality many years later in the Islamic Republic of Iran Army with a cut-down Spartan mounting an indigenously produced Fadjr 1 107mm rocket launcher. In the Iranian army, the CVR(T) family is known as Tosan, meaning Wild Horse or Fury.

5,465kg and it had a payload of 3,000kg. The basic vehicle had a flat deck and offered two front configurations: one with a lightweight cab structure that was unarmoured, while the other incorporated full armour protection for the driver and engine compartment. The introduction of the HMLC followed the memorable appearance of Erica Roe at the England v Australia rugby union match at Twickenham on 2 January 1982. Being essentially a topless Spartan, the vehicle was named Streaker. By 1984 two prototypes of the Streaker were built. These underwent trials with the Royal Engineers and were purchased by the MoD. The role of the HMLC was subsequently subsumed into the Stormer family.

RIGHT **A Stormer HVM SP of 9 Battery 12 Regiment Royal Artillery takes part in an Exercise MedMan at BATUS in May 2005. The Starstreak HVM system entered service with 12 and 47 Regiments Royal Artillery in 1997. Currently, 12 Regiment is equipped with 36 Stormer firing platforms in 3 batteries – T (Shah Shujah's Troop), 9 (Plassey) and 58 (Eyre).**

Starstreak

In June 1982, Alvis released outline drawings for 14 variants based on the chassis of the Stormer platform. In the summer of 1986, the British Army selected the Stormer as the carrier for the Shorts Starstreak HVM air defence system. The High-Velocity Missile system is a low-level Close Air Defence (CAD) system with a rapid engagement capacity designed to destroy helicopters and Close Air Support aircraft. The missile employs a

LEFT **The Stormer HVM SP system carries eight ready-to-fire missiles with a further eight reloads. The Starstreak II missile has a speed of 3.5 Mach to a range of 7,000m. It is also effective against AFVs because of its high kinetic energy.**

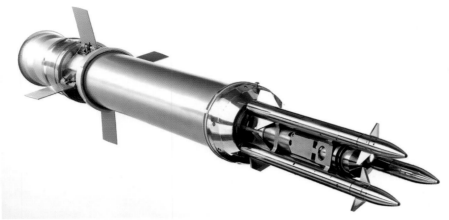

system of three dart-type projectiles. Each of these darts has an explosive warhead ensuring high lethality against any aerial target. Mounted on the turret roof to the right of the commander's cupola is the Avimo acquisition sight and mounted between the two banks of four Starstreak missiles is the passive Thorn EMI Air Defence Alert Device. The first of 156 Stormer HVM SP systems entered service with the British Army in 1997.

Shielder anti-tank minelayer

Prior to the outbreak of the Gulf War in February 1991, the British Army issued an Urgent Operational Requirement for a mobile, tracked mine-dispensing system to create anti-tank barriers rapidly. Six vehicles based on the Stormer armoured flatbed chassis incorporating the Giat Minotaur AC F1 dispenser were produced within 14 weeks under the designation Vehicle Launched Scatterable Mine System or VLSMS. Four were deployed to the Gulf by air just before the land campaign began. The Minotaur system was capable of laying an anti-tank minefield 2.5km long in under five minutes. After the war, the British Army wished to retain such a capability. Trials were conducted between the original French Minotaur, the German Skorpion Minenwerfer and the US Alliant Techsystems M-163 Volcano system. The latter was chosen in 1995 and four years later, now

named Shielder, entered service with the Royal Engineers at a cost of £110million for 29 vehicles. The Volcano dispensed only anti-tank mines as the British Army no longer utilises anti-personnel mines on the battlefield. The Shielders were deployed on Operation Telic in 2003 and subsequently withdrawn from service in 2014.

Life-extension programme

One of the reasons for the failure of the Mid-Life Improvement Programme for CVR(T) in 1979 was the expectation that the FV100 series would be replaced by a new family of AFVs known as TRACER. When this also came to naught, CVR(T) had to carry on regardless. In time, the British Army experienced increasing engine problems that were described by cavalry officers of the 9th/12th Lancers and 13th/18th Royal Hussars – the two armoured reconnaissance regiments in BAOR – as 'chronic'. On occasions, up to 40% of Scorpions and Scimitars were off the road for various lengths of time depending on the supply of spare parts. Complete troops of four vehicles had

ABOVE A Shielder fires a canister of six Bombs HE No 2 Mark 1 from the M-136 Volcano delivery system that is capable of laying an anti-tank barrier of up to 960 mines within minutes.

BELOW A Scimitar DSL (E-SPIRE) of the Combined Arms Training Centre takes part in an exercise on Salisbury Plain Training Area (SPTA).

been withdrawn from field exercise for want of engine replacements in some instances. The British Army examined the idea of replacing the Jaguar J60 with a Perkins Diesel T6.3544 as part of a CVR(T) mid-life fleet update but decided against it. Prevarication was no longer an option.

The first installation of a Perkins T6.3544 in CVR(T) was carried out in 1980 by Alvis to meet a foreign requirement for a diesel option. This vehicle installation was developed at Alvis to British Army standards and tested to meet worldwide conditions. Following successful in-house proving, Alvis commissioned the ATDU at Bovington to conduct two 10,000-mile proving trials to provide an independent seal of approval for export customers. These trials achieved their objective and also gave the British Army first-hand experience of the engine. The vehicles used for these trials were then demonstrated extensively overseas, providing further confirmation of the engine's reliability under the harshest conditions, particularly in the Arabian Gulf and Sweden.

In 1985, a diesel-powered Scorpion was loaned to the 13th/18th Royal Hussars by Alvis to assess its performance in typical BAOR conditions. During Exercise Winter Canter in the Harz Mountains, the vehicle performed all standard reconnaissance tasks, despite encountering the most severe weather for 25 years in western Germany, achieving universal approval from the regiment. A feasibility study undertaken by No 38 Central Workshops at Chilwell indicated that the cost of installing the Perkins T6.3544 would be £15,500 per vehicle. The estimated life cycle cost benefit of dieselisation was deemed to be £26,830 over a 15-year period assuming an average of 2,000km running per annum. Year-by-year analysis of the alternative costs of petrol and diesel engine installation showed that the break-even point, when the additional dieselisation costs were fully recovered from operational savings, occurred in the fourth year after overhaul. The full saving over 15 years would therefore be in the order of £18million for the complete CVR(T) fleet based in BAOR.

Even so, it took another decade before the MoD decided to implement such a necessary improvement under the CVR(T) Life-Extension Programme (LEP). In 1998, a £32million production contract was awarded to Alvis Vehicles Ltd for the manufacture of 1,107 conversion kits for most variants of CVR(T). The first delivery was completed on schedule in April 1999 and thereafter the whole fleet was modified at the rate of approximately 25 vehicles a month. ABRO Donnington also undertook some 600 LEP conversions. The engine chosen

RIGHT ANDROMEDA, a Samaritan DSL Bowman of A Squadron, 1st Royal Tank Regiment, stands by during an exercise on SPTA.

for the conversion was the Cummins BTA5.9 turbocharged diesel engine developing 190bhp coupled to a modified David Brown Defence TN15E+ gearbox giving significant increases in reliability, durability, range and safety. The diesel engine gave the Scorpion a maximum road speed of 50mph (80kph) and a road range of 600 miles (870km).

Just as important were the improvements to the surveillance capability of CVR(T) with the installation of SPIRE (Sight Periscopic Infra-Red Equipment) TI systems. The first of these were deployed to Bosnia for the Scimitars of the British SFOR (Stabilisation Force in Bosnia and Herzegovina) vehicles under an Urgent Operational Requirement. The British Army version of SPIRE was called E-SPIRE but subsequent types developed by Thales included the second generation (M-SPIRE) and a stabilised version (U-SPIRE).

ABOVE A Scimitar DSL BGTI Bowman of C Squadron The Household Cavalry Regiment, displays the prominent Battle Group Thermal Imaging sights for the commander and gunner during Exercise Iron Scout 3 in 2016.

In August 2001, a major contract of £230million was awarded to Thales for the British Army's comprehensive Battle Group Thermal Imaging (BGTI) programme. These new TI sights were installed in 361 Warrior IFV and 146 Scimitars to give both AFVs the capability to engage targets at longer ranges and under almost all weather conditions. The BGTI sights incorporated a laser rangefinder for accurate range assessment, as well as flat-panel displays for both commander and gunner that also provided access to Bowman communications and battle management systems. A further update was the Tactical Navigation Target Location System (TNTLS)

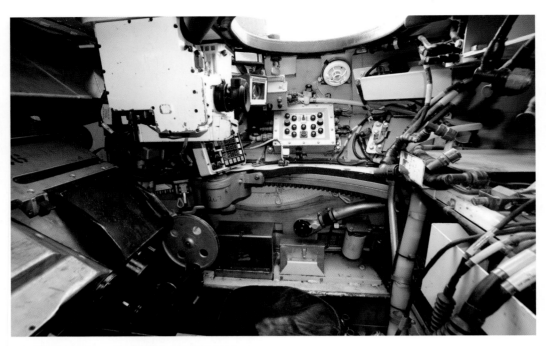

RIGHT AND BELOW
A Scimitar DSL
BGTI Bowman
shows the gunner's
position (right) and
commander's position
(below) with their much
enhanced Battle Group
Thermal Imaging sights.

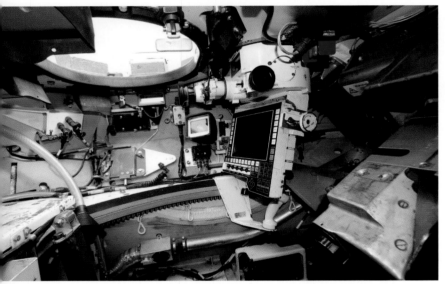

that also allowed the commander to guide the driver with a read-out in his instrument panel.

Following operational experience in the Balkans where the greatest threats to CVR(T) were mines, the British Army demanded additional passive armour to enhance protection. Although not part of LEP, a Mine Blast Protection (MBP) of belly armour and Ballistic Protection (BP) programme was introduced in 2005. The armour upgrade of MBP and BP was only applied to Scimitar, Spartan and Samson vehicles. With continuing service in Iraq and Afghanistan, MBP2

provided further protection that, all together, included all-round bar armour against RPG and HEAT attack; appliqué armour to hull and turret for increased protection against small-arms fire and kinetic attack; mesh guards for turret sights; and turret wire cutters.

A more mundane development to the CVR(T) fleet was the substitution of the original Armstrong suspension dampers with Messier hydraulic units giving a 25% improvement in cross-country mobility and greater crew comfort on the move. This was introduced after the Gulf War of 1991 when CVR(T) suffered unpleasant ride characteristics due to the ridged nature of the desert terrain. These dampers were fitted during base overhaul over the years, although most crews stated they could not tell the difference between the two.

While the unbearable Middle East summer heat never materialised during the Gulf War of 1991, that certainly proved to be the case in both Iraq and Afghanistan where daytime temperatures were often in excess of +40ºC. In 2009, the CVR(T) Environmental Mitigation (EM) upgrade package was introduced for the vehicles serving on Operation Herrick in Afghanistan. This provided several enhancements for the Cummins powerpack in the appalling weather conditions, from the extreme heat of summer to the freezing depths of winter in the desert. Provision for the crew

LEFT In order to increase firepower in Afghanistan, a number of Spartan 2s were fitted with the Odin turret armed with the Browning .50-calibre heavy machine gun. The M2 HMG Odin turret was developed by AEI Systems and has a sensor pack on its right-hand side.

was limited to spot-cooling for the commander and gunner, while the driver had a cooling vest before a comprehensive air-conditioning system was fitted in place of the NBC pack. As always, such modifications came at a price, both monetary and more importantly by weight. The weight of Scimitar had now risen from 7,800kg to 12,250kg with all the associated implications for mobility and reliability.

Scimitar 2 and Spartan 2

The continuing campaigns in Iraq and Afghanistan took a heavy toll of wear and tear on CVR(T), let alone the ever-present threat of ambush and IEDs. In December 2010, the MoD awarded a £30million contract to BAE Systems for a further comprehensive upgrade of CVR(T) known as Project Transformer. In essence, this represented completely new CVR(T) Mark 2 variants based on Scimitar, Spartan, Samaritan, Sultan and Samson. A total of 58 vehicles were initially upgraded to the Mark 2 standard with the first batch comprising 30 Scimitars, 9 Spartans, 4 Samaritans, 2 Sultans and 2 Samsons. The first of them were flown to Afghanistan in late August 2011 for use by the 9th/12th Royal Lancers with 3 Commando Brigade during Operation Herrick 14.

The Mark 2 configuration featured a new,

better-protected aluminium hull with greater internal volume. All the crew was now provided with blast-attenuating seats for improved survivability in case of mine strike. Both versions were fitted with the latest armour package as well as a full suite of electronic countermeasures. The Scimitar Mark 2 utilised the existing 30mm Rarden turret but the commander and gunner were provided with the Thales M-SPIRE. The same new chassis was used for the Samson Mark 2 and Spartan Mark 2 while Samaritan and Sultan had a new hull with a raised roofline for their more particular roles.

ABOVE A Scimitar Mark 2 TES or Theatre Entry Standard is loaded at RAF Brize Norton on its first deployment to Afghanistan in August 2011.

In April 2013, a further safety device was introduced for the commander and gunner on Scimitar Mark 2 vehicles with the Roll-Over Protection Structure (ROPS), which as its name implies reduces casualties should the CVR(T) overturn. The final modification of note was the installation of the Enforcer Remote Weapon System on Spartan Mark 2 to allow sustained machine-gun fire from under armour.

THE DEMISE OF SCORPION

During the late 1980s, health and safety concerns arose over the level of toxicity to crew members within the turrets of Fox, Scorpion and Scimitar when firing for prolonged periods. Crews had always suffered from skin irritation due to cordite when the breech was opened after firing, but had found means to ameliorate the situation by either leaving the BV going (so the steam carried the cordite particulates upwards through the open hatches) or else setting the NBC system to 'Level One' so that the overpressure achieved the same function. In a trial held at the Gunnery School at Lulworth in November 1991 the levels of toxicity were measured scientifically to determine the Short-Term Exposure Level (STEL) of various noxious compounds, including carbon monoxide, hydrogen chloride, hydrogen sulphide, hydrogen cyanide and ammonia that were generated within the vehicles. The trial indicated that Scorpion was the worst offender with levels from hydrogen chloride, hydrogen sulphide and hydrogen cyanide exceeding the STEL. The powers that be decreed that Scorpion must be withdrawn from service but not Scimitar.

Intriguingly, this decision coincided with the provisions of the Conventional Armed Forces in Europe (CFE) Treaty between NATO and the Warsaw Pact implemented in 1990. It was intended to establish specific limits on key categories of conventional military equipment from the Atlantic to the Urals. At Russia's insistence, all AFVs with a main armament greater than 75mm were to be classified as a 'tank'. Accordingly, Scorpion fell into this category with its 76mm gun. At the same time, it allowed thousands of obsolete PT-76 amphibious light tanks to be included in the overall number of 'tanks' to be scrapped under CFE. Therefore, it was logical to dispense with Scorpion to preserve the number of MBTs within the British Army. Vladimir Putin repudiated CFE in 2015.

Other armies equipped with 76mm-armed Scorpions did not deem it necessary to follow the British example. Since then the British Army has sought to blame the RAF Regiment as being the instigator of Scorpion's withdrawal from service because of toxicity, but by the time of the Lulworth trial the decision had been taken to retire all their CVR(T) variants from the RAF because their role was now deemed to be superfluous to requirements following the collapse of the Soviet Union.

CVR(T) production and foreign sales

The CVR(T) range of combat vehicles was manufactured by Alvis Limited of Coventry. Total production was 3,716 vehicles of which many were exported to foreign armies. These included the armed forces of Belgium (701), Botswana (60), Brunei (16), Chile (30), Honduras (19), Iran (250), Indonesia (90), Ireland (14), Jordan (69), Malaysia (26), New Zealand (26), Nigeria (150), Oman (120), Philippines (7), Spain (17), Tanzania (40), Thailand (154), Togo (12), United Arab Emirates (76) and Venezuela (78).

PRODUCTION FIGURES

Scorpion 76 (1,241), Striker (132), Spartan (967), Samaritan (101), Sultan (372), Samson (136), Scimitar (486), Scorpion 90 (32), Stormer (249).

ABOVE Both Australia and Canada procured Scorpion turrets to create Fire Support Vehicles based on the M-113 APC and Cougar chassis respectively. The latter is part of the Canadian Armoured Vehicle General Purpose family and this pair of Cougar FSVs is taking part in the combined NATO Exercise Rendezvous 83. The Cougar is no longer in service except in reserve units.

RIGHT The Irish Army procured 14 Scorpions between 1980 and 1985. It entered service with 1st Tank Squadron in March 1980 in a distinctive camouflage scheme of black, brown and green. Standard modifications included the mounting of 0.50 calibre Browning machine gun on the turret roof and latterly a fume extractor for the 76mm gun to reduce toxicity within the turret. The Scorpion was withdrawn from service in 2017.

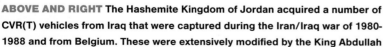

ABOVE AND RIGHT The Hashemite Kingdom of Jordan acquired a number of CVR(T) vehicles from Iraq that were captured during the Iran/Iraq war of 1980–1988 and from Belgium. These were extensively modified by the King Abdullah II Design and Development Bureau in a number of projects that were intended for the export market. The main improvements were the fitting of a 194bhp Steyer M16 diesel engine and new transmission. Several turrets were also designed with the main armament comprising a Ukrainian ZTM-1 30mm cannon, as well as the 130mm Barrier ATGW for the innovative Kastet with its one-man (as above right). A modernised Spartan was the only CVR(T) variant to enter Jordanian service with the Darak Gendarmerie (as above left).

Chapter Seven

CVR(T) in RAF service

The Royal Air Force Regiment was the other major user of CVR(T) in British service between 1982 and 1992. Their role was for the defence of air bases in RAF Germany and across the world. In particular, CVR(T) gave close protection for the Harrier Force in RAF Germany when it deployed to temporary air strips in support of NATO forces through much of the Cold War.

OPPOSITE '**Exit right! Exit right!**' **Gunners of the Royal Air Force Regiment disembark from a Spartan APC as they secure the perimeter of an airfield against enemy incursion.** *(RAFHM)*

RAF Light Armour Squadrons

ABOVE The Royal Air Force was an early adopter of armoured cars, arguably as far back as 1914 with the use of Rolls-Royce armoured cars by the Royal Naval Air Service. During the 1920s the RAF employed armoured car companies in the Middle East to protect their widespread airfields in the region, from Egypt to Iraq – the progenitors of the RAF Regiment Light Armour Squadrons with CVR(T). (RAFHC)

The Royal Air Force Regiment was formed with the sole purpose of providing close defence of RAF airfields. The concept arose after the fall of France in 1940 when the German strategy of deep-penetration Blitzkrieg demonstrated the vulnerability of airfields long considered safe, being deep behind friendly lines. In February 1942, the RAF Regiment was created by Royal Warrant as an integral part of the Royal Air Force. The defence of airfields lay in a combination of RAF Regiment gunners manning light anti-aircraft (LAA) weapons to counter air attack and field squadrons equipped with armoured cars to patrol well beyond the airfield perimeter to prevent ground infiltration. By the end of the war in 1945 the RAF Regiment had grown to over 80,000 men. In the post-war years, the role of airfield defence remained paramount with squadrons scattered across the world from the Azores to Hong Kong and from Germany to the Falkland Islands. The venerable Bofors 40mm L60 and L70 LAA

RIGHT The Royal Air Force Regiment received its first CVR(T), Spartan APC 48AT02, on 19 August 1991 at RAF Catterick.

guns were superseded by the Rapier SHORAD SAM system. Similarly, ground vehicles such as the Ferret armoured car and the Land Rover were dramatically upgraded in 1981 by the procurement of 150 CVR(T)s for the RAF Regiment.

At the time, the RAF Regiment comprised 11 regular squadrons and the Royal Auxiliary Air Force Regiment. Six of these were rerolled as Light Armour Squadrons with CVR(T) comprising No 1 Squadron, No II Squadron (2, but always in Roman numerals), No 15 Squadron, No 34 Squadron, No 51 Squadron and No 58 Squadron. Each squadron was equipped with 23 CVR(T)s including Scorpion, Spartan, Sultan, Samaritan and Samson. In 1984, the RAF Regiment established a Light Armour Training Squadron (LATS) at the Corps Depot at Catterick to provide formal training for Light Armour Squadrons. Ordinarily, four LASs were based in the UK under the command of No 1 Group within Strike Command. The latter was also responsible for No 34 LAS based in RAF Akrotiri in Cyprus with a single flight of four Spartans and two Scorpions, while the remainder of its CVR(T)s were kept in the UK. One LAS was always deployed in RAF Germany with the Harrier Force and another at RAF Laarbruch under the command of 33 Wing.

The Light Armoured Squadron (LAS) was organised into a Squadron Headquarters with one Sultan in HQ Flight and one Samson in the Engineer Flight, together with three Spartan Flights, each of 5 Spartans and 35 gunners, and the Scorpion Flight of 6 Scorpion 76mm FS, giving a total of 23 CVR(T)s in each LAS. This changed depending on the tactical situation; thus a composite counter-attack force could comprise two Scorpions and four Spartans or any variation deemed necessary. It soon became apparent that the Spartan was not suited to carrying two crewmen and five troops in the back with all their kit. Accordingly, one gunner was deleted from each Spartan and became a four-man 'brick' in Land Rovers for added flexibility, acting as covert OPs, long-distance patrolling or supporting dispersed Rapier SAM detachments beyond the airfield perimeter. The final ORBAT of LAS took some time to realise.

In times of heightened tension, Light Armour Squadrons were to be deployed to Germany to provide protection to the major strike airbases of RAF Bruggen, RAF Laarbruch and RAF Wildenrath, as well as RAF Gütersloh, with two further squadrons devoted to the support of the Harrier Force on its mobile deployments at dispersed airstrips across BAOR. The defence of RAF Akrotiri in Cyprus was the responsibility of No 34 Squadron. In time of war, all Light Armour Squadrons were committed to RAF Germany, while regular peacetime exercises, such as Gazelle Arabian '85 and '87, were conducted on an annual basis given the many other commitments of the regiment. In addition, the menace of international terrorism and civil disobedience against military targets remained a constant, notably at RAF

ABOVE Prior to the issue of their own CVR(T)s, the troops of the Light Armour Squadrons undertook training with army vehicles but they maintained their own identity by applying RAF roundels to the front hulls of the Scorpions.

RIGHT AND BELOW
One of the fundamental roles of the Light Armour Squadrons in RAF Germany was the protection of the Harrier Force while on its dispersed deployments across the country.

Greenham Common and protecting Aldergrove Airport in Belfast.

The principal threats in RAF Germany were assessed to be Soviet airborne and heliborne forces equipped with their integral AFVs, such as the ASU-85 assault gun and the BMD-1 armed with a 73mm 2A28 Grom gun and Sagger ATGW, as well as Spetsnatz saboteurs. For these reasons, CVR(T) with its greater firepower, mobility and armour protection was a necessary adjunct to RAF Regiment troops in LWB FFR Land Rovers. There is no question that the RAF Regiment would have preferred Scimitar instead of Scorpion as the 30mm Rarden gun was better suited to the potential Soviet AFVs that the LASs were likely to meet. However, a cancelled order for CVR(T) Scorpions by the Al Khomeini regime after the fall of the Shah of Iran dictated otherwise. In time of war, the 76th Guards Chernigov Airborne Division was tasked with assaulting RAF Bruggen, RAF Laarbruch and RAF Wildenrath. A project study revealed that even if the combined total of all the anti-tank ammunition and weapons within a Light Armoured Squadron scored a first-round direct hit, together with initial reloads, there would still be a 30% deficit against the number of Soviet air-landed AFVs. In the words of Josef Stalin – 'Quantity has a quality all of its own.'

Operation Corporate

The first two Light Armoured Squadrons were No 1 and No II Squadrons, both because of their seniority and the fact that they formed the original RAF Armoured Car Companies in the Middle East during the 1920s. The RAF Regiment No II Squadron also has the distinction that its personnel were parachute trained for rapid deployment. Preparations for the new role began in 1979 with selected personnel attending courses at the RAC Centre at Bovington, so by 1982 a cadre of CVR(T) expertise had been created. In February, II LAS completed its gunnery training at Lulworth followed by a Tactical Firing Camp package at Castlemartin ranges in South Wales during May. It was fitting that these events coincided with the 60th anniversary of the squadron's formation as an Armoured Car Company of the Royal Air Force on 7 April 1922. There was no time, however, for celebrations as Argentine forces had invaded the Falkland Islands on 2 April 1982 and the RAF Regiment was immediately tasked with providing SHORAD Rapier

BELOW Driver training was undertaken under the auspices of the Light Armour Training Squadron at the Corps Depot at Catterick in Yorkshire.

ABOVE A brand-new Scorpion stands on display at RAF Catterick in the distinctive RAF camouflage of black over brown stripes. The RAF Regiment procured a total of 186 CVR(T)s including Scorpion, Spartan, Sultan, Samaritan, Samson and Scimitar.

detachments to join the Naval Task Force despatched to the South Atlantic.

On 18 May 1982, No II Squadron LAS was ordered on standby to deploy with Light Armour. This was just one month after the official date that the squadron had become operational as a Light Armoured Squadron. On the following day, a meeting was held at HQ Strike Command to discuss the detailed planning for the deployment of a complete Light Armoured Squadron and for a potential parachute deployment on to the Falklands. With 2 and 3 PARAs already on the Falkland Islands, No II Squadron was the only available airborne unit in the UK as 1 PARA was on internal security duties in Northern Ireland. This coincided with the Battle of Goose Green where 2 PARA won a famous victory but suffered 15 killed and 30 wounded, mainly due to a lack of fire support that could have been provided by CVR(T). The possibility of deployment by air was just what CVR(T) had been designed for initially but it was not to be, though not for the want of trying as the squadron diary reveals:

We were in the hangar three times, drawn, fitted and checked. Twice we were at Lyneham with everything and once we were lined up behind the C-130. ... The first time was almost certainly a dry run. The other two occasions, as far as we knew in mushroom land were weather wave-offs. The third time was definitely the intent to go.

As one Gunner recalled: 'I do know I was lined up behind a Charlie 130 in June 1982 expecting to climb aboard with my final destination as Port Stanley airport.' Instead, No II Squadron was sent to Northern Ireland on yet another roulement tour of Operation Banner. The capture of Port Stanley was rapidly forgotten on the grimy streets of Belfast.

LEFT A complete Light Armour Squadron at RAF Honington prepares to move out on exercise. The LAS was organised into a Headquarters Flight, an Engineer Flight, three Spartan Flights and a Scorpion Flight, with a total of 23 CVR(T)s.

RAF Akrotiri, Cyprus

In the name of God, the merciful, the compassionate, the United Nasserite Organisation announces that the three martyr groups carried out their mission successfully and, according to plan, inflicted heavy damages at the British–US–Zionist base [RAF Akrotiri, Cyprus]. The three groups were able to destroy a number of helicopters, jetliners and transport planes. They also destroyed accommodation of the British families inside the base.

On Sunday 3 August 1986, a terrorist attack was launched on the British Sovereign Base Area of RAF Akrotiri in retaliation for the US bombing of Libya on 15 April 1986. Codenamed Operation El Dorado Canyon, the raid itself was a reprisal for the deaths of US service personnel in a West Berlin discotheque ten days earlier. Accordingly, No 34 Light Armour Squadron was on high alert throughout the early summer with hull-down positions prepared at every gate of the airbase for the Scorpions, while Spartans and Land Rovers patrolled the perimeter.

On Friday 1 August, the state of high alert was relaxed for the first time and the Scorpion guarding ARABS (Akrotiri Rowing and Board Sailing) Gate was withdrawn in the afternoon. Flight Sergeant Bill Elspie noticed that the chain and padlock securing the gate were rusty, so he called in at the stores department just as it was closing for the weekend. All that was available was a length of aircraft lash-down chain and a Chubb padlock of industrial proportions. In the afternoon of Sunday, the first weekend of the Cypriot national summer break, three Hotchkiss Brandt 60mm mortar bombs were fired into the airbase, one of which slightly wounded Mrs Eileen Malpass near her married quarters. Simultaneously, three terrorists tried to shoot off the padlock at ARABS Gate by Kalashnikov fire with absolutely no success. Instead, they turned their guns on the ARABS beach club and its car park. By a remarkable coincidence, the children of Mrs

ABOVE AND BELOW A Samson ARV undertakes the recovery of a Spartan APC during an exercise on the Yorkshire Moors. A single Samson was attached to the Engineer Flight of each Light Armour Squadron.

Malpass were in the car park with Mrs Sandra Edwards when the firing started. Rebecca Malpass, aged eight, showed great bravery and presence of mind by running out, under fire, to drag her two-year-old brother into a car and lie protectively above him, while Mrs Edwards was injured by bullet fragments. The Education Officer, John Lancaster, was also in the car park with his father's brand-new BMW 323. One of the terrorists fired a complete AK47 magazine at him from a distance of just 20yd but only a single bullet struck the car.

By now the airbase was on full alert and the Quick Reaction Force, on two-minute standby under the command of Flight Lieutenant Mike Bird, was deployed in Land Rovers to all the other gates. Flight Sergeant Bill Elspie, the CVR(T) flight commander, rushed to the command centre in his whites and batting pads from an interrupted cricket match where he found Wing Commander Hugh Cross, the

RIGHT The RAF's Explosive Ordnance Disposal Squadron was formed in 1943 to defuse German bombs and by 1945 it had rendered safe some 176,000 aerial weapons. Since June 1995, 5131 (Bomb Disposal) Squadron was based at RAF Wittering in Cambridgeshire with the responsibility for the disposal of all air delivered weapons across the United Kingdom. The unit was disbanded in 2020.

BELOW No 5131 (Bomb Disposal) Squadron employed the FV103 Spartan APC and the FV107 Scimitar. The Spartan acted to carry EOD operators and their specialised equipment, including quantities of plastic explosive to disrupt or destroy unexploded ordnance. This EOD Spartan was stationed at RAF Mount Pleasant on East Falklands where unexploded munitions remained in abundance after the conflict in 1982. Note the Bomb Disposal insignia on the front and the red-painted hull corners that was common to all RAF EOD vehicles. This gave rise to their nickname of Red Wings.

deputy station commander, directing operations. A legendary name within the RAF (whose godfather was Douglas Bader), Cross called to Elspie and stated: 'Bill, send the CVR(T)s to the armoury now and get a full bomb load and when you get to the Scorpions I want at least ten fucking rounds of canister in each turret.' Other terrorists were firing indiscriminately towards the crowded beaches but again without inflicting casualties. Fortunately, the attack subsided quickly as the terrorists fled in the face of marauding Scorpions and Spartans. The total number of casualties were two middle-aged women slightly injured and two terrorists wounded. The main attack was to have been through ARABS Gate with a pick-up truck loaded with RPGs that were to be used against the bulk tanks of JP7 aviation fuel. A stout padlock and good contingency planning thwarted the raid completely. The Duchess of Kent presented Rebecca Malpass with the Child of Courage Award for 1986.

An EOD operative attaches an RE61 Rocket Wrench to the nose of a Mark 82 500lb bomb in order to remove the fuse during a training exercise with a Spartan in the background.

Operation Granby

Following the invasion of Kuwait by Iraq in August 1990, British forces deployed to Saudi Arabia to forestall any further of Saddam Hussein's expansionist ambitions in the region and subsequently to liberate Kuwait from the Iraqis. The requirement for the defence of airfields in the Middle East immediately increased, leading to the deployment of RAF Regiment Squadrons to the region as part of Operation Granby. Although the RAF Regiment's manpower amounted to only 3% of the RAF's overall strength, it provided 16% of the support with some 12 of the RAF Regiment's 19 combat units involved in the Middle East. First and foremost were SHORAD Rapier units, followed by Light Armour Squadron with No 34 deploying from RAF Akrotiri to Bahrain and Dhahran airbases for perimeter defence. In January 1991, No 1 Squadron, together with their CVR(T)s, were flown from Germany to Muharraq in Bahrain. With only three days' notice, they were replaced by No 58 Squadron just before the air war began and redeployed to Al Qaysumah in Saudi Arabia. From there, their CVR(T)s moved into the desert and provided close defence for the support helicopter squadrons operating in the forward areas along the Kuwaiti border. During Operation Desert Sabre, the CVR(T) of No 1 Squadron provided close protection to the support helicopter squadrons operating with the ground forces and as part of the divisional flank protection screen.

It is fitting that No 1 Squadron finished the war across the Basra–Kuwait highway in the last operation conducted by CVR(T) with the RAF Regiment. Its antecedent unit, No 1 Armoured Car Company, was originally formed in December 1921 for service across the Middle East. The company protected RAF airfields in Egypt and Mesopotamia while assisting with law enforcement duties across the region, from RAF Haifa in Palestine to RAF Hinadi in Iraq. Following the collapse of the Soviet Union and the diminishing threat to RAF bases in Germany, the CVR(T) fleet was withdrawn from the Order of Battle of the RAF Regiment in 1992.

'THE FASTEST TANK IN THE WORLD'

The *Guinness Book of Records* states that 'the fastest production tank in the world' is a Scorpion. On 26 March 2002 an S2000 Scorpion Peacekeeper achieved a speed of 51.10mph (82.23km/h) at the Qinetiq test-track at Chertsey in Surrey. Given that the Scorpion Peacekeeper was not a production vehicle, few CVR(T) crewmen would recognise such a paltry speed. Many would claim to have driven faster.

An unladen Striker was clocked at 70mph by a police VASCAR speed camera on the A303, while an RAF Regiment Spartan was observed travelling at 73mph on the A1 – unfortunately by the crew's wing commander in a following staff car.

So the record goes to the RAF Regiment on both road and test-track since the Engineer Flight of 15 LAS extensively modified one of their Scorpions. Christened 'Flash the Tank', it achieved a speed of 84mph on the main runway at RAF Hullavington to become the fastest tracked vehicle in the world.

ABOVE The high speed of the CVR(T) family demanded caution when travelling on public roads. This was instilled in drivers during their training.

BELOW The Royal Air Force Regiment claims the title for the fastest tracked vehicle in the world when a modified Scorpion driven by SAC Neil Robinson achieved a speed of 84mph.

Chapter Eight

CVR(T) on Peace Support Operations

It is of interest to note that the majority of CVR(T)'s overseas deployments were on Peace Support Operations under a United Nations mandate in a role for which it was never intended. Yet its versatility in far-flung places, from the Balkans to Afghanistan, showed it to be highly effective in this capacity given that 'Peace keeping is not a job for a soldier, but it is a job only a soldier can do'.

OPPOSITE Eternal vigilance was the name of the game during Peace Support Operations in the Balkans where knowledge of the dispositions and intentions of the warring factions was essential in order to protect the benighted civilian populace and allow reconstruction to proceed.

ABOVE The dead of an ethnic cleansing atrocity are stacked aboard a Samaritan CVR(T): just one of many distasteful tasks for UN personnel in their peacekeeping efforts in the Balkans.

Operation Grapple – Bosnia-Hertzegovina, 1992

The Delhi Spearmen

The CVR(T) was first deployed on Peace Support Operations in the Former Republic of Yugoslavia in November 1992 as part of the First Cheshire Battle Group committed to the United Nations Protection Force (UNPROFOR). There is no space in this account to explain the wars fought in 1992 to 2001, both between Yugoslavia's former constituent republics and by the murderous alphabet soup of self-declared nationalist/ religious entities which sought – sometimes by the most barbarous methods – to alter the map of its populations in a brutal and genocidal campaign of 'ethnic cleansing'. The multifarious warring factions were consumed by visceral hatred for each other and few gave any credence to the 'blue berets' tasked with implementing UN Security Council Resolution 776 of 14 September 1992.

The principal aim of the UN Resolution was to provide safe passage for humanitarian aid convoys to reach the civilian populations displaced by the civil war. The British battalion group (BRITBAT) was deployed to central Bosnia on 1 November 1992 some 18 hours by tracks or trucks from its main supply base at the port of Split. During Operation Grapple 2, BRITBAT comprised 1st Battalion The Cheshire Regiment with its 46 Warrior Infantry Fighting Vehicles and 8 CVR(T) Scimitars of its integral Reconnaissance Troop. Since reconnaissance on the ground was such a vital task for the formation, it was supplemented by a cavalry squadron of 26 CVR(T)s of B Squadron, 9th/12th Royal Lancers – The Delhi Spearmen. These comprised Scimitar,

RIGHT One of the major assets of CVR(T) was its ability to negotiate most of the primitive road system and reach remote villages so as to show the UN flag and provide humanitarian aid as required.

Spartan, Sultan, Samaritan and Samson types to undertake a wide range of tasks across the area of operations (AO).

It was soon apparent that CVR(T) was well suited to the UNPROFOR role since its light weight made it capable of travelling across most of the primitive road network, whereas the 28-ton Warrior was often defeated by the weak bridges designed for the age of the horse and cart. Furthermore, the CVR(T) was less belligerent in appearance than Warrior despite the same main armament. This was particularly so with the Spartan APC armed with just a machine gun. Routinely carrying local interpreters, it often opened negotiations with villagers or at checkpoints to allow safe passage for UN humanitarian convoys. The reassuring presence of the Samaritan armoured ambulance ready to dispense medical aid as required also ameliorated the powerful company of AFVs.

The initial task of CVR(T) was to reconnoitre the complete road network within the AO to create a 'going' map for all manner of vehicles and, in particular, the Warrior IFV, so that it could be readily deployed to any potential confrontation point between the warring factions. Herculean efforts by the Royal Engineers over the winter of 1992 – the worst on record since 1911 – repaired and created roads and tracks that were negotiable by AFVs, while numerous bridges were reinforced or replaced. With its squadron base at Vitez, the 9th/12th Lancers were now able to range far and wide in their reconnaissance role, aided by the newly introduced studded winter track that gave much-enhanced traction on ice, together with the bags of grit carried by every vehicle. The other primary role for the Lancers was escort duty for convoys plying between Zenica and Tuzla: a distance of about 50 miles as the crow flies, lengthened and complicated

ABOVE Sergeant John Clarke stands in the turret of his Scimitar 08FD02 Callsign Three One that fired the first shots in anger by CVR(T) during a Serb ambush of an aid convoy in February 1993.

ABOVE The primary role of Operation Grapple was to provide succour to civilians caught up in the bitter civil war with humanitarian aid convoys escorted by the AFVs of BRITCAVBAT.

BELOW A solitary Scimitar of The Light Dragoons maintains an Observation Post in a monotonous duty undertaken in all weathers and all hours in the name of peace.

by narrow country roads in the hills, particularly when hampered by deep winter snow and treacherous ice.

BRITCAVBAT
The Light Dragoons

As part of Operation Grapple 2, B Squadron, The Light Dragoons, replaced B Squadron, 9th/12th Royal Lancers, in May 1993. It was the first operational tour for the newly formed regiment of The Light Dragoons following the amalgamation of the 13th/18th Royal Hussars (Queen Mary's Own) and the 15th/19th The King's Royal Hussars on 1 December 1992. B Squadron was attached to the 1 Prince of Wales's Own Regiment of Yorkshire (1PWO) Battle Group. The squadron comprised 101 Dragoons manning four Sabre troops with one of four Scimitars and the three others each having three Scimitars and one Spartan. The latter provided the all-important personnel-carrying capability, typically a medic and an interpreter.

Other components were Squadron Headquarters, the Administrative Troop and the Fitter Section. At this time in the campaign, few modifications had been carried out on

CVR(T) beyond each troop having at least one vehicle fitted with a VHF/HF radio, while the provision of handheld GPS receivers increased during the deployment. An Urgent Operational Requirement was submitted by the regiment for a five-point harness for CVR(T) drivers in order to ameliorate blast and associated injuries should the vehicle hit a mine.

The primary role remained the escort of humanitarian aid convoys to civilians displaced by the war but it is estimated that anything up to 80% of the aid was appropriated by the warring factions to be sold on the black market and thus fund their nefarious activities: criminality being just as important a motivation as nationalism.

Similarly, UNPROFOR was supposed to act as a neutral balance between the various militias but each side accused it of siding with the enemy, so being named derisively as SERBPROFOR or HVOPROFOR. Since firm political direction from the UN remained lacking, the troops on the ground instituted more robust measures with the 1PWO Battle Group gaining the reputation of 'SHOOTBAT' in their quest to protect the civilian populace. In the words of Lieutenant Colonel Alastair Duncan, the CO of 1PWO:

ABOVE The relatively innocuous appearance of CVR(T) Spartan as compared with the formidable Warrior was exploited for transporting personnel when negotiating passage between the different warring factions.

BELOW Much to the chagrin of their crews, orders from above often forbade the flying of national flags or regimental pennants on AFVs depending on the political situation. This aid convoy is reduced to a UN flag but the black and white 'South African Flash' (from the 13th/18th Royal Hussars) on the commander's upper arm indicates that this Scimitar is from C Squadron, The Light Dragoons, as part of the Augmentation Force in 1994.

Our UNPROFOR mandate was quite clear – get food and aid through to people who required it from the border with Croatia all the way to Tuzla. It was a huge task for one battalion but we got all the aid through, thousands and thousands of tonnes of it. In terms of keeping people alive during a war, we were hugely successful.

Throughout 1993 and into 1994, The Light Dragoons provided the armoured reconnaissance elements of successive battle groups until it became a regimental entity itself with two squadrons and RHQ deployed in Bosnia-Herzegovina. Dubbed BRITCAVBAT or British Cavalry Battalion, it operated out of bases that encompassed Tuzla, Tomislavgrad, Vitez, Žepče, Gornji Vakuf and Maglaj, along with a host of smaller field locations. AOs spread from the south-west to the north-east of central Bosnia and ended up in the 'Maglaj Finger', surrounded on three sides by the Bosnian Serbs. Constant patrolling was the order of the day with CVR(T) able to reach any spot in the AO that often eluded the heavier and wider Warrior IFVs. Indeed,

Warrior became increasingly unpopular with the local communities due to the damage to roads and bridges. This situation became worse in winter due to Warrior's necessarily aggressive winter track. For this reason, CVR(T) assumed more of the latter's roles with ever-increasing mileages.

It is tragic to relate the majority of UN casualties and most fatalities were due to road traffic accidents. Even so, enemy fire from all the various factions, but particularly the Bosnian Serb Army (BSA), was a constant threat ranging from small arms and anti-aircraft guns to tank fire by BSA T-72 MBTs and even FROG missiles that caused craters 30ft across by 10ft deep. Furthermore, British soldiers kept respirators close to hand in northern Bosnia given that the BSA had stockpiled chlorine gas on the front lines. The order of battle of opposing troops in northern Bosnia contrasted markedly with that found in the country's central region where Croatian HVO soldiers and Muslim BiH troops were fighting each other as well as the Bosnian Serb Army, whereas in the north, Croat and Muslim armies fought side by side against the Serbs.

BELOW One of the hallmarks of operations in Bosnia-Herzegovina was the need for endless patience when dealing with the warring factions in a machismo society where any man with a Kalashnikov at a checkpoint was a potential killer, particularly when fuelled by slivovitz.

The Dragoons' responsibilities included escorting humanitarian aid convoys along the infamous 'Bomb Alley' between Kjadanj and Stupari. The area ran close to the Serbian front line and was frequently shelled. Convoys from Belgrade under Operation Cabinet were escorted three times a week across the front line on their way to the United Nations High Commissioner for Refugees (UNHCR) warehouse at Lukovac. This facility had to be guarded to prevent looters and even other UN contingents purloining supplies that were deemed to be, in the jargon of the time, 'non-swimmers' within UNPROFOR. Another task for B Squadron was to monitor and reconnoitre the whole of the northern Bosnia area. These intelligence-gathering missions provided an opportunity to fly the UN flag and created a presence in areas not frequently visited by the UNPROFOR. By these means, the humanitarian requirements of isolated communities could be passed to headquarters for action as necessary. Keen knowledge of the ground is part and parcel of being a cavalryman.

ABOVE A Samaritan of B Squadron, The Light Dragoons, takes part in Operation Cabinet on 19 May 1993 when a major UNHCR convoy from Belgrade was escorted by the squadron across the Serbia/Bosnia Inter-Entity Boundary Lines.

BELOW A Scimitar of The Light Dragoons at the Glamoc gunnery ranges tests the new gunner's SPIRE sight acquired under an Urgent Operational Requirement.

Household Cavalry Regiment 1994, 1996, 1999

Staff Corporal Henry Newton, The Lifeguards, served in all three deployments:

The role was drastically different each time. In 1994 it was United Nations. At the time I was a trooper, just a driver with the troops. There was still a lot of ethnic cleansing going on. We tried to monitor it as best we could, and stop it happening but obviously with the United Nations, there was only so much you could do and you had to stand back, being under the law where you could only fire if you were fired upon. Otherwise you would get dragged into it yourself. Our Squadron had Scimitar. It was very difficult. Lots of poverty, lots of orphans. Which for a young trooper was a bit of an eye-opener. We used to get supplies to them but the supplies disappeared before they got to us. Also any building we did for schools, again stuff was taken.

For the next tour in 1996 we were in Banja Luka at the wood factory as an independent squadron. Our main task was at a place where refugees of all ethnic groups in Bosnia went. One of our missions was to try to sustain that village with resupply, help them through the winter, such as getting logs from the woods. Help them as best we could. Lots of hearts and minds: playing football with the kids; getting to know the locals. In the period of time that I'd been away it had got a lot better. I was the troop leader's operator so I gained a different perspective. With knowledge, the mission becomes clearer for you. It was a very good tour.

For the UN tour we were in white vehicles and sky-blue berets. It took a bit of getting used to. For the second tour we were in the British Army green and black with regimental add-ons.

With the first tour we were far more stand-offish. There were lots of Mujahideen who didn't like us being there. They wanted to get about their business. On the first tour we used to get stoned by the kids. On the second tour we used to pull up and all the kids would have prepared a makeshift football pitch because they knew that we played football. We played a lot of football. I didn't come away being David Beckham, but by the end our skills were a lot slicker than at the beginning. We also provided protection within the town of Banja Luka. In the town centres there were lots of people going around with small arms and anything could kick off at any time, and so it was policed. We were working a lot with the local police trying to get them to do the business. But there was a lot of corruption. In 1999 the tour was again completely different. We were taking out foot patrols but in a very relaxed posture. You'd go up to get a coffee, mingle with the locals and they liked that.

Peace Support Operations were to continue in Bosnia-Herzegovina until 2019 through Operation Resolute with the NATO Implementation Force (IFOR) replacing UNPROFOR and then Operations Lodestar and Palatine with SFOR in 1997 comprising 39 different countries, which had the mission of 'peace enforcement'. Finally, the European Union Force Bosnia and Herzegovina was formed in December 2004 in order to police the region under Operation Althea and detain possible war criminals. Between 1992 and 2019, 59 British soldiers were killed in Bosnia and many more injured. Throughout that time, the CVR(T) played a prominent part in the cause of peacekeeping.

BELOW With SFOR emblazoned on all quarters, a Scimitar passes a ruined building, so commonplace across Bosnia-Herzegovina, in 1997. The vehicle is named ARTHRITIS; that seems appropriate for a vehicle in its 25th year of service with the British Army.

Operation Agricola – Kosovo, 1999

The field of blackbirds

With internecine warfare raging across the various states of former Yugoslavia during the 1990s, the people of the Serbian province of Kosovo became increasingly restive. Since 90% of the population was ethnic Albanian, the yoke of rule from Belgrade was evermore irksome, leading to the formation of the Kosovo Liberation Army or KLA. As attacks on Serbian security forces grew so the latter's repression of the population mounted, leading to the flight of hundreds of thousands of refugees to the neighbouring countries of Albania and Macedonia during the bitter winter of 1998. Despite entreaties from the international community, the Serbian forces of Slobodan Milošević continued their cruel prosecution of ethnic cleansing.

In February 1999, a NATO peace implementation force, known as Kosovo Force

(KFOR), was created. Eventually 40,000 NATO troops were deployed to the region with over 4,000 of them from the British armed forces. On 24 March, NATO unleashed a bombing campaign against military targets in Kosovo and Serbia itself. Serbian obduracy persisted unabated, leading to a further refugee crisis as a million Albanians sought safety outside Kosovo. Finally, diplomatic pressure and the accumulative destruction of Serbian infrastructure from aerial bombardment forced President Milošević to order a military withdrawal from Kosovo on 9 June 1999. This allowed the deployment of KFOR to oversee it.

The British Army's commitment to KFOR began in February 1999 under the codename of Operation Agricola. Two battle groups of 4th Armoured Brigade were formed around the Irish Guards in Warrior IFVs and the King's Royal Hussars in Challenger 2 MBTs, together with artillery, engineer and aviation assets. Force reconnaissance was provided by D Squadron of the HCR mounted in CVR(T)s

ABOVE A Stormer HVM SP is directed aboard a C-17A Globemaster 2 prior to a flight to Macedonia at the outset of Operation Agricola.

with Scimitar, Spartan, Sultan, Samaritan and Samson variants. At the time, the HCR was committed to Operation Palatine as part of SFOR in Bosnia-Herzegovina with the best CVR(T) vehicles deployed with B and C Squadrons.

Accordingly, the remaining Scimitars were in urgent need of refurbishment, exacerbated by the requirement of fitting M-SPIRE, then being introduced for the turret crew. Unfortunately, the team tasked to do so mistakenly installed the sights on some vehicles that had been rejected for deployment on KFOR. It was too late to rectify the situation before D Squadron flew to Thessaloniki in Greece to collect their vehicles that had been sent ahead by ship.

As the train carrying D Squadron departed for Macedonia to join 4th Armoured Brigade, it was intercepted by an anti-NATO demonstration. In the words of the HCR journal:

When we trundled out of the port at two o'clock in the morning late-night revellers staggered out of the cafés to hurl abuse at us and the occasional rocks through the windows of the train. The scene was more macabre than intimidating. The Squadron's reaction was merely to curl up and sleep on the seats or the floor of the train, like bored lions in a cage that could strike at any moment should they so wish. This nonchalant approach infuriated the Greeks, especially the film crews who had arrived looking for some action.

Departure was delayed but training soon began in earnest at a former Yugoslav army camp at Krivolak. At the end of May, the squadron moved to Skopje Airport with a troop deployed on the Macedonia/Kosovo border. There it was possible to view the unrelenting bombing strikes against Serbian targets. There was still no indication of a Serbian withdrawal from Kosovo so there remained the prospect of spending the summer in sweltering temperatures with no political resolution. However, before leaving Krivolak a barbecue was held, at which the guitar-playing Lieutenant James Blount (the now-famous musician James Blunt) sang his latest tune 'Kosovo! Here We Go!' Fortunately, the words never really deviated from the title so everybody was able to sing along. For Lance Corporal Adams, finding room on his Scimitar Three Zero for Lieutenant Blount's guitar was always a problem: 'We got his guitar in the back bin, which was a bit of a struggle, but when we all got together, I'd light a fire and we'd do a song. I had no idea he was going to become a famous pop star.'

BELOW The Red Dragon on the hull front of this Scimitar indicates the Welsh Cavalry or 1st The Queen's Dragoon Guards as part of IFOR in 1996. The fundamental purpose of UN forces in the Balkans was to allow reconstruction of the shattered infrastructure following years of vicious civil war.

Kosovo! Here we go!

On 12 June 1999, the battle groups of 4th Armoured Brigade entered Kosovo with D Squadron HCR leading along the main axis of advance through the strategic Kaçanik Gorge. The latter was seized in a helicopter assault by the Parachute Regiment and 1 Gurkha Rifles, as were vital bridges in a highly successful reprise of Operation Market Garden. The road to the Kosovan capital of Pristina was open. As troop commander of 3 Troop, Lieutenant James Blount's Scimitar was at the forefront of the advance as his driver, Lance Corporal Adams, recalls:

We were the lead callsign. At my level initially, as a lance corporal, we were somewhat in the dark – we didn't know if we were going to be on a war footing or peacekeeping. I well remember going through Macedonia with the crowds cheering and shouting 'NATO'. And then as we went on to the road that took us into Kosovo there was a refugee camp. All the children came running down the hill towards the fence line, cheering. Our main jobs were securing the roads, to allow the militias to leave Kosovo itself. So we were lining routes, just making sure they were leaving. That lasted for about four weeks.

On entering one village all the children and adults clustered around the vehicles and threw roses and chocolates on them.

The days when soldiers are showered with flowers as liberators are few and far between.

There are several claims as to which British Army unit first entered Pristina. It was in fact a CVR(T) Samaritan of HCR that became detached and drove through the streets of the city, alone and lost.

Of course, Special Forces (SF) had been operating in Pristina previously. The priority target was the airport and at 1800 hours on 12 June 1999, D Squadron escorted the Paras there only to find it occupied by a Russian motorised rifle company. A stand-off ensued as high-level negotiations took place to prevent a military confrontation. Again, Scimitar Three Zero was in the thick of the action as Lieutenant Blount recalls:

I was the lead officer with my troop of Scimitars. I was given the direct command [from NATO commander General Wesley Clark] to overpower the 200 or so Russians who were there. The soldiers directly behind me were from the Parachute Regiment so they were obviously game for the fight. . . . Fortunately, up on the radio

LEFT Ecstatic crowds greet the CVR(T)s of the Irish Guards Battle Group on Saturday 12 June 1999 as it advances along the road to Pristina, the capital of Kosovo.

177

came General Mike Jackson, whose exact words at the time were, 'I'm not going to have my soldiers be responsible for starting World War III', and ordered us to encircle the airfield instead. After a couple of days the Russians there said 'We have no food and no water so can we share the airfield with you?'

Fortunately, conflict was avoided, and the withdrawal of Serbian forces went mostly according to plan. A week later, the squadron was given a Tactical Area of Responsibility comprising a stunningly beautiful rural area of some 400km^2, running from Pristina up to the eastern boundary with Serbia. The remaining three months of the tour were spent patrolling the hills while acting as a 'tripwire' to any Serb insurgency back into Kosovo, as well as creating a secure environment in which the Albanian and the minority Serb communities could start to reconstruct their lives. Ironically, having been greeted as liberators by the oppressed Albanians, the British Army was obliged to protect the Serbian minority from revenge attacks. An eye for an eye remains a way of life and death in the Balkans.

Operation Herrick – the Fourth Anglo-Afghan War

'Those who cannot remember the past are condemned to repeat it.'

The words of the Spanish philosopher and poet George Santayana ring so true when it comes to Britain's ultimately futile wars in Afghanistan. Suffice to say, it was the British armed forces that paid an awful price in blood, mutilation and mental anguish in the Fourth Anglo-Afghan War of 2002–14. The first

CVR(T) vehicles were employed on Operation Herrick 4 when D Squadron of the HCR was deployed as the Formation Reconnaissance Squadron with 16 Air Assault Brigade in 2006. It was a return to the Middle East for D Squadron following their earlier attachment to 16 Air Assault Brigade during Operation Telic and the invasion of Iraq in 2003.

While acclimatising at Camp Bastion the squadron fitted Plasan plates and bar armour to their 'wagons' for greater protection against small-arms fire and RPG weapons. The squadron comprised four Sabre Troops with three Scimitars and one Spartan APC apiece. Support to battle group operations took the form of securing helicopter landing sites, lines of departure and securing or holding ground for infantry and logistic assets, as well as CVR(T)'s attributes of fire and movement.

For the squadron, operating in the height of an Afghan summer was extremely uncomfortable and punishing to both men and vehicles, as was shown while providing an armoured screen in support of a Regional Task Force plan during July. The task itself was uneventful, but the heat took its toll on both vehicles and men, the most serious of whom, Trooper Goodyear, was a near fatality, with an inner core temperature of 107°F (41.7°C). Environmental health officers subsequently visited the tank park to ascertain the heat levels within the vehicles, but as it was morning they got a reading of

only 128.4°F, nowhere near the 158°F in the drivers' compartments operated in from June to early August. The largest threat to the squadron came from landmines either washed down the wadis or Soviet legacy mines littering the desert. D Squadron suffered six mine strikes but fortunately with no fatalities. Nevertheless, throughout its activities with the Mobile Operations Group, the CVR(T) vehicles provided rapid mobility, firepower and protection for the battle group and brigade. They were now an essential component of COIN operations in Afghanistan.

Herrick 8

This level of success was certainly not experienced when D Squadron HCR returned to Afghanistan in 2008 for Operation Herrick 8. By now, the CVR(T) had been in theatre for almost 18 months without overhaul through broiling summers and freezing winters. The harsh environment of the Afghan 'dasht' or desert, extreme heat then extreme cold, the fine sand and the unforgiving rough and rocky terrain and vast distances covered had all taken their toll. As an independent Formation Reconnaissance Squadron attached to 16 Air Assault Brigade once again, D Squadron was soon struck down by repeated breakdowns. In the first two months, the CVR(T) fleet covered just 270km during which the LAD changed 17 engines, 12 gearboxes, 19 fan assemblies and 22 starter motors. By contrast, D Squadron

ABOVE Scimitars of D Squadron, HCR, negotiate the dasht of Helmand Province at speed during Operation Herrick 8 in June 2008.

ABOVE After the fitting of the enhanced armour package, the next modification of note in Afghanistan was the addition of ECM and ECCM devices to detect and disrupt IEDs or Improvised Explosive Devices that became ever more sophisticated and, therefore, dangerous to AFVs.

RIGHT A Scimitar Bowman of D Squadron, HCR, displays the later version of the ECM and ECCM equipment with IR disruptors above the front track guards as it traverses waterlogged ground during Operation Herrick 13 in 2011.

travelled 34,000km during Operation Herrick 4 with only six engine changes and four gearbox failures in four and a half months.

As a case in point, when the squadron deployed in May to Musa Qa'leh just 85km from Camp Bastion, the journey took three days rather than one, due to the number of repairs necessary en route. During the 72 hours, the Fitters Section had no sleep at all and the return trip was just as bad when 17 out of the 30 vehicles broke down. Not only was D Squadron's tour badly disrupted, but the previously excellent reputation of CVR(T) had been badly sullied. CVR(T) had a proven track record in Helmand. It had always offered precision firepower, good mobility over most terrain in most weather with excellent day and night surveillance capability. Yet the threat of IEDs had become a major obstacle and danger to all Coalition vehicles in the country. The reputation of Formation Reconnaissance was steadily deteriorating and Tactical Support Vehicles such as Jackal and Bulldog ATVs were no real substitute.

Fortunately, the problems had been addressed through a whole series of Urgent

Operational Requirements known as EM enhancements. Vehicle reliability was the priority with a new air intake snorkel and filter to reduce dust ingestion; a new uprated clutch more suited to the characteristics of the Cummins diesel engine; an improved aluminium radiator and charge air-cooling; transmission heat exchanger with a fuel-cooling system incorporated into the powerpack; a starter thermal override; and an engine temperature gauge for the driver to monitor performance. The original TN15 gearbox was sequentially upgraded to TN15E+ standard coupled to improved final drives as fitted to Stormer. Since the weight of Scimitar had risen from 7.8 tons to around 11, stronger torsion bars and suspension dampers were fitted to restore mobility, as well as an improved braking system. These enhancements were known as CVR(T) Phase Two Upgrade that were collectively referred to as Operation Pilton by the many participating companies, although this was not an official designation. During 2009, 102 CVR(T)s upgraded to this standard were deployed to Afghanistan. Force Reconnaissance was back in business.

ABOVE The Scimitar 2 and Spartan 2 were first employed in Afghanistan by the 9th/12th Royal Lancers in September 2011 during Operation Herrick 14. The many upgrades to CVR(T) meant a new designation depending on its state – whether it be engine, armour protection or radio fit. Thus the full designation of O6FD46 opposite was Combat Vehicle Reconnaissance Full Tracked Scimitar DSL (235) (E-SPIRE) Mine and Ballistic Protected 30mm Gun Bowman. It is therefore impossible to give the full designation for every CVR(T) for reasons of space.

Herrick 16

Operation Herrick was now a heavy commitment for all the Formation Reconnaissance Regiments beside the Household Cavalry Regiment – 1st The Queens Dragoon Guards (1QDG), 9th/12th Royal Lancers and The Light Dragoons. When not deployed in Afghanistan, these units and their CVR(T)s were committed to Operation Telic and the ongoing campaign in Iraq. Each Operation Herrick brought its own problems for troops and their equipment. With increasing casualties, Force Protection became ever more important and that was reflected in the many modifications made to CVR(T) throughout successive Operations Herrick, culminating in the Scimitar and Spartan Mark 2 models. It fell to A Squadron of The Light Dragoons to be the last Force Reconnaissance Squadron

BELOW Before and after a mine strike on a Scimitar 2 of The Light Dragoons: one of the last CVR(T) casualties of the conflict. The crew survived.

operating across Helmand Province on Operation Herrick 16 in 2012, following the regiment's previous deployments on Herrick 5, 6 and 10. By the end of April, A Squadron had deployed to Mobile Operating Base Price where it undertook the takeover from the outgoing 1QDG Formation Recce Squadron.

Tragically, the QDG lost two men when a CVR(T) overturned following a mine strike. In response, the ROPS turret-top cage was developed and fitted soon after the arrival of The Light Dragoons. In the words of the regimental EME (Electrical and Mechanical Engineer) officer, it made, 'the sleek and slender CVR(T) come to resemble a Dalek on steroids'. The new configuration presented extra problems with the main one being a lack of stowage: the perennial problem with CVR(T). The extra weight often required the crews to fit

new tracks every 200 miles or so and the turret traverse gearboxes also had to be changed frequently because of the extra weight of the turret. But most frustrating of all were the ever more proscriptive rules of engagement in the use of the 30mm Rarden, even when the enemy was actively undertaking nefarious activities.

Operations began with three Sabre troops on CVR(T) Scimitar 2, one support troop on Spartan 2 and a Force Support Group troop mounted in Jackal Tactical Support Vehicle (TSV). SHQ was equipped with Jackal and Husky FSV with an attached troop on Coyote. With this ORBAT, the squadron undertook a couple of operations before everything was thrown into chaos when most of the squadron was redeployed to the thankless task as Afghan police advisers. Months of Mission-Specific Training were cast aside. This reduced A Squadron to just two Sabre troops to undertake Force Reconnaissance operations with a concomitant much-increased workload. The squadron's main areas of operations were to the north of the task force area in the Upper Gereshk Valley with Combined Force Burma under control of the 2 Royal Welsh Battle Group. Operations continued throughout September and October until the handover to the Queen's Royal Lancers. The latter part of the tour was dominated by the recovery of personnel and equipment, including all the CVR(T) vehicles, from Afghanistan to UK where The Light Dragoons returned in November. Herrick 16 was the last operational deployment of CVR(T). It had served the British Army well, from the Falkland Islands in 1982 to Afghanistan in 2012, in some 30 years of combat operations.

BELOW The Light Dragoons deployment on Operation Herrick 16 marked the end of hostilities for CVR(T) in Afghanistan. As of December 2020, The Light Dragoons are going to war again in CVR(T) with their deployment to Mali under Operation Newcombe.

Epilogue

CVR(T) – the end of the line

LEFT After 50 years of service with the British Army, the CVR(T) has reached the sunset of its life. Its effectiveness over so many years was out of all proportion to its size. Most of all it won the abiding affection of its crews despite its foibles. Nevertheless, CVR(T) will live on for many years as it remains the AFV of choice for collectors.

RIGHT No account of CVR(T) is complete without acknowledgement of the contribution played by the Royal Electrical and Mechanical Engineers in maintaining the vehicles under every condition of adversity to allow the force commander to have as many vehicles serviceable as possible for combat operations.

BELOW A machine is but the sum of its parts and without its human crew it has no life or purpose. The CVR(T) crews of the RAC cavalry regiments believe themselves to be a breed apart in their role of Close and Medium Reconnaissance that requires a special aptitude and commitment to fulfil their vital function in the prosecution of armoured warfare.

ABOVE The development of Scimitar and Spartan Mark 2 marked a fundamental increase in combat power, particularly in the peculiar operating conditions of Afghanistan and Iraq. The many modifications did much to improve crew survivability – and therefore morale – throughout those difficult campaigns. 62KM65 was the prototype Spartan Mark 2.

ABOVE Despite years of service in the Middle East, the Scimitar Mark 2 also comes in green for operations in temperate climes, as with this Scimitar Mark 2 during Operation Cabrit – the NATO Enhanced Forward Presence in the Baltic States. The full designation for this vehicle is Combat Vehicle Reconnaissance Full Tracked 30mm Gun Scimitar Mark 2 (SPIRE).

ABOVE It is fitting that the first regiment to be equipped with the Ajax family of six variants is the Household Cavalry Regiment that was first to receive Scorpion in 1972. Flanked by two Scimitars is the ARES version all flying the regimental flag of HCR. The ARES is the Protected Mobility Recce Support vehicle designed to carry seven specialised combat troops on the battlefield.

RIGHT The Ajax family is no direct replacement for CVR(T) but more as a successor. Whereas CVR(T) was born out of the quest for light armour in the 1960s, Ajax introduces the concept of medium armour. At 42 tonnes, the Ajax reconnaissance and strike vehicle weighs six times that of Scorpion and is armed with an innovative CTA1 40mm CTAS (Cased Telescoped Armament System) capable of accurate firing on the move. Medium armour represents a quantum leap forward in battlefield capability.

Index